DIAGNOSING ORGANIZATIONS

Third Edition

Applied Social Research Methods Series
Volume 8

APPLIED SOCIAL RESEARCH
METHODS SERIES

Series Editors
LEONARD BICKMAN, Peabody College, Vanderbilt University, Nashville
DEBRA J. ROG, Vanderbilt University, Washington, DC

DIAGNOSING ORGANIZATIONS

Methods, Models, and Processes

Third Edition

Michael I. Harrison

Applied Social Research Methods Series
Volume 8

SAGE Publications
Thousand Oaks ■ London ■ New Delhi

For information:

Sage Publications, Inc.
2455 Teller Road
Thousand Oaks, California 91320
E-mail: order@sagepub.com

Sage Publications Ltd.
1 Oliver's Yard
55 City Road
London EC1Y 1SP
United Kingdom

Sage Publications India Pvt. Ltd.
B-42, Panchsheel Enclave
Post Box 4109
New Delhi 110 017 India

Library of Congress Cataloging-in-Publication Data

Harrison, Michael I.
Diagnosing organizations: methods, models, and processes / Michael
I. Harrison.—3rd ed.
      p. cm.— (Applied social research methods series; v. 8)
Includes bibliographical references and index.
ISBN 978-0-7619-2571-2 (cloth) — ISBN 978-0-7619-2572-9 (pbk.)
   1. Organizational behavior. 2. Organizational change. I. Title. II. Series.
HD58.7.H3697 2005
302.3′5—dc22

                                                      2004009245
Printed on acid-free paper in the United States of America.

              08   09   10   9   8   7   6   5   4   3   2

Acquiring Editor:	Lisa Cuevas Shaw
Editorial Assistant:	Margo Crouppen
Production Editor:	Tracy Alpern
Copy Editor:	Dan Hays
Typesetter:	C&M Digitals (P) Ltd.
Indexer:	Gloria Tierney
Cover Designer:	Janet Foulger

In memory of my father, Milton S. Harrison
In celebration of the arrival of Romy, our newest family member

Contents

Preface

In the decade since publication of the second edition of this book, several trends have emerged that make diagnosis of organizational problems and challenges even more crucial for change management than in the past. Businesses and even some not-for-profit organizations face increasingly uncertain operating conditions and stiff competition at home and abroad. Major business consulting firms have expanded their services in change management. Within firms, managers with technical or business backgrounds, rather than specialists in human resources and planned change, are leading ambitious reorganizations, implementing new technologies, and changing management practices. These changes seek dramatic improvements in productivity, competitiveness, and quality. Without careful diagnosis of organizational conditions and reasoned choice of change mechanisms, consultants and managers risk imitating fashionable management techniques that may not suit the focal organization and can even harm it. Similarly, when managers forge strategic alliances and introduce information technologies that are attractive from a business standpoint, they also need to assess how well these moves fit the less visible human features of their organizations, such as reward systems, culture, work practices, and cross-functional coordination.

In this edition, I try to show how diagnosis can help managers and consultants act quickly and flexibly to meet the challenges of uncertain environments, changing goals, new technologies, stiff competition, and tight budgets. The book retains the format of earlier editions and the three-way focus on diagnostic methods, models, and processes. However, I thoroughly updated the contents to reflect developments in the business and organizational settings in which diagnosis takes place, current practices in diagnosis, and trends in change management. I also made changes that reflect the evolution of my own thinking about diagnosis, much of which is presented in *Organizational Diagnosis and Assessment: Bridging Theory and Practice* (Harrison & Shirom, 1999). From that book comes a new emphasis on ensuring that diagnosis directly addresses the problems and concerns that are critical to clients, rather than just providing general feedback on current operations.

The following are a few specific departures from earlier editions. The process of using and constructing diagnostic models and frames, which was previously called interpretation, is now called *modeling*. The terms *framing* (e.g., of diagnostic problems) and *analysis* (e.g., of diagnostic findings) are also substituted for what was previously called *interpretation*. The open systems model in Chapter 2 has been modified to improve clarity. Goals and strategies are no longer included in the system model but are treated as important reference points in diagnosis. A simpler and more commonsense definition of technology is used. The discussion of effectiveness criteria has been updated and expanded, with greater emphasis on the benefits of diagnosing sources of ineffectiveness. Chapter 3 contains a revised treatment of the model for diagnosing individual and group behavior and a new discussion of Hackman's Action Model for Group Task Performance. Chapter 4 contains revised discussions of strategic alliances among organizations, lateral coordination and cross-functional teams, and divisionalized firms; a new section on combining opposing principles of organizational design; and greater attention to uses of information technology. In Chapter 5, six guidelines for environmental relations assessment replace the 10 diagnostic guidelines contained in the second edition. SWOT (strengths, weaknesses, opportunities, and threats) analysis is presented as a distinctive technique, which can contribute both to analysis of competitive strategy and to broader forms of diagnosis. References to research have been kept to a minimum in the chapters. Reviews of relevant theories and research are readily available in annual publications, recent texts, and handbooks (see Appendix D). The appendixes and references have all been revised and updated. Appendix B now includes references to several models from which important diagnostic instruments derive. Web addresses are provided for sources of instruments (Appendix B) and professional and academic organizations (Appendix D).

My work on this and earlier editions of this book benefited from ideas and feedback from students at Bar Ilan University and the School of Management at Boston College; exchanges with managers and consultants with whom I worked in The Netherlands and Israel; and the supportive and collegial work environments provided by Bar Ilan, Boston College, and Harvard Business School. I acknowledge the contribution of my colleague Arie Shirom to my understanding and work on diagnosis. In addition, thanks are due to the following people, who encouraged my work and helped me craft my ideas: Thomas Backer, Peter Bamberger, Jean Bartunek, Yaacov Ben Dor, Leonard Bickman, Sarah Edom, Ephraim Golan, Judy Gordon, Nisan Hadas, Jo-Ann Harrison, the late Ed Huse, the late Dafna Izraeli, Jan Jonker, Ronit Kark, Bruce Phillips, Debra Rog, Yizhak Samuel, Moshe Stillerman, Bill Torbert, Arthur Turner, and Izik Uno. Michael Beer, Richard Hackman, Brigette Schay, and Andrew Van de Ven provided helpful information on instruments described in Appendix B. Ettie Rosenberg prepared the book's figures.

This edition of the book was completed while I was on leave from Bar Ilan University and serving as a senior research scientist in the Center for Delivery, Organization, and Markets (CDOM) at the Agency for Healthcare Research and Quality (AHRQ) in Rockville, Maryland. I thank Irene Fraser, CDOM's director, for supporting the project. The book's contents do not represent the views of the agency. Thanks to the staff of AHRQ's Information Resources Center for their assistance. Finally, I acknowledge the enduring encouragement and support of my wife, Jo-Ann.

1

Diagnosis: Approaches and Methods

This chapter examines the main features of diagnosis and its uses in consultations for organizational improvement and change. Three critical facets of diagnosis are introduced: (a) *process*—working with members of an organization to plan a diagnostic study, administer it, and provide feedback on the findings; (b) *modeling*—using models to frame issues, guide data gathering, identify organizational conditions underlying problems, and organize feedback; and (c) *methods*—techniques for collecting, analyzing, and summarizing diagnostic data.

In organizational diagnosis, consultants, researchers, or managers use conceptual models and applied research methods to assess an organization's current state and discover ways to solve problems, meet challenges, or enhance performance.[1] Diagnostic practice applies ideas and techniques from a diverse range of disciplines within behavioral science and related fields, including psychology, sociology, management, and organization studies. Diagnosis helps decision makers and their advisers develop workable proposals for organizational change and improvement. Without careful diagnosis, decision makers may waste effort by failing to attack the root causes of problems (Senge, 1994). Hence, diagnosis can contribute to managerial decision making, just as it can provide a solid foundation for recommendations by organizational and management consultants.

The following are two examples of the use of diagnosis in consulting projects in which I took part:[2]

Case 1

In cooperation with the chief personnel officer in a branch of the armed forces, a human resources unit prepared a survey of organizational climate and leadership in field units. Repeat applications of the survey tracked developments within units over time and provided comparisons between functionally similar units at the same point in time. Members of the human resources unit provided commanding officers with periodic feedback containing both types of data. The feedback helped officers recognize problematic leadership and administrative practices and motivated them to take steps to improve these practices.

Case 2

The head of training in a national health maintenance organization (HMO) received a request from the director of one of its member organizations—here called Contemporary Health Facility (CHF)—for an ambitious program that would train CHF employees to undertake a major organizational transformation. The transformation proposed by the director would radically redefine the goals and mission of CHF. Moreover, it would alter CHF's patient characteristics, personnel, size, structure, and its relations with other health-care organizations. The director of CHF was worried that his nursing staff and administrative employees would oppose the far-reaching changes he envisioned. Unconvinced that the training program was justified, the head of training in the HMO reached an agreement with the CHF director to ask an independent consultant to assess the situation. After discussions between the consultant, the head of training, and the top managers at CHF, all parties agreed to broaden the study goals to include assessment of the feasibility of the proposed transformation and the staff's readiness for the change. Training was to be considered as only one possible step that might facilitate the transformation.

Over a period of 3 weeks, the consultant conducted in-depth interviews with CHF's 3 top managers and 7 staff members who held positions of authority. In addition, he conducted focus group interviews with 12 lower-level staff members; made site visits; and examined data on CHF's personnel, patient characteristics, and administration. The consultant analyzed and presented these data within the context of a guiding model of preconditions for strategic organizational change. This model drew concepts from research on open systems, organizational politics, and leadership for organizational transformation. The major diagnostic finding was that the transformation was both desirable and feasible, but accomplishing it would be risky and difficult. In his report and oral feedback to the CHF management and the HMO's director of training, the consultant conveyed these conclusions and some of the findings on which they were based. Moreover, the consultant recommended steps that the director of CHF could take to overcome opposition and build support for the proposed transformation of CHF and suggested ways of implementing the transformation. The report also recommended ways to improve organizational climate, enhance staffing procedures, and improve other aspects of organizational effectiveness with or without implementing the program to transform CHF.

Diagnostic consultations such as the ones just described often begin when clients ask for advice from consultants. The main clients for a diagnosis are the people who bear most of the responsibility for receiving feedback, deciding what to do about it, and launching actions in response to it. These people are usually the ones who originally solicited and sponsored the study, but responsibility for sponsorship of a diagnosis and use of its findings may be divided:

In both Case 1 and Case 2, a national-level manager initiated the diagnosis, but heads of operating units (i.e., the commanders of the military field units and the director of CHF) were expected to act on the feedback. Clients for diagnosis are often top administrators, as in the two cases presented previously. However, union management teams (Shirom, 1983), midlevel managers, entire working groups, owners, and supervisory agencies can also act as clients. In some change projects, special steering committees are set up that are parallel to, but outside of, the operating hierarchy of the organization (Rubenstein & Woodman, 1984). These steering groups define project goals, plan interventions, and supervise project implementation.

Clients play a critical role in defining the consultation's goals (see Chapter 6) and shaping relations between consultants and the focal organization. In the cases described previously, the clients turned to consultants trained in the behavioral sciences because the clients assumed that their organization's problems and challenges related to people, groups, and organizational arrangements rather than involving mainly business or technical issues. Clients seeking help managing and changing organizations often refer initially to problems such as the following:

- Poor quality, delays, crises, and other signs of ineffectiveness
- Declining demand or revenues, client/customer dissatisfaction, and criticism by external stakeholders
- Human resource problems, such as rapid employee turnover, stress and health problems, and low morale after downsizing; difficulties managing a multicultural workforce
- Challenges posed by radical changes in markets and government regulation
- Difficulties making major transitions—from family to professionally managed firms, mergers, reorganizations
- Trouble starting or completing complex projects (e.g., implementing new technologies and establishing product development teams)

In other instances, clients want an assessment of how well the organization functions in a specific area, such as staff development (e.g., Case 6, which is presented in Chapter 3). Also, they may seek advice on improving processes such as quality assurance or customer service. Such concerns have led to consultations and change projects in public-sector organizations, such as schools, hospitals, city governments, and the military; private firms in areas such as manufacturing, banking, and retailing; voluntary groups, including charities and religious groups; and cooperative businesses and communities.

The consultants (or practitioners) who specialize in planned change and applied research often develop skills in giving feedback and working with teams as well as in investigating and analyzing operating problems and challenges. These consultants can be located in external consulting agencies or universities, or they can act as internal consultants, who come from organizational units specializing in areas such as human resource management, quality, planning, or evaluation (McMahan & Woodman, 1992). In many instances, internal specialists in change come from fields such as information systems, industrial engineering, strategy, and marketing rather than behavioral science. Moreover, a growing body of business consultants now act as specialists in change management (Worren, Ruddle, & Moore, 1999), whereas other external consultants contribute expertise in particular industries or functional areas, such as information technology. Top executives and even middle managers and other line managers often drive changes in strategy, structures, staffing, technology, and culture. These managers may draw on specialists to facilitate change, but line managers retain responsibility for the overall direction and execution of the project (Kanter, Stein, & Jick, 1992; Sherman, 1995).

In many diagnoses, as in Case 2, the consultant conducts a diagnosis to understand the nature and causes of the problems or challenges initially presented by clients, identifies additional organizational problems and opportunities, and seeks ways to solve these problems and improve organizational effectiveness.[3]

Both of the previous cases involved the common diagnostic practice of comparing the current state of the client system with some preferred state— improved relations between officers and subordinates in Case 1 and provision of a wider range of health services by a more professionalized staff in Case 2. Each of these diagnostic studies involved a search for ways to narrow gaps between the current and desired states. The consultants also assessed effectiveness in terms of a standard (e.g., ratings of officers in comparable units).

In light of the diagnostic findings, consultants often point to the need to change one or more key features of the organization, such as its goals, strategies, structures, technologies, or human resources. Moreover, consultants may recommend a wide range of steps (interventions) that management or other clients can undertake to bring about the desired improvements. Clients sometimes ask the practitioners who conducted the diagnosis or other consultants to help them implement these steps toward improvement.

USES OF DIAGNOSIS

Diagnosis can contribute to many types of consultations for organizational change. The following sections compare its use in different types of change projects.

Diagnosis in Organization Development and Change Management

Diagnosis plays a role in both organization development (OD) projects and business-oriented change management projects. OD, which includes action research and planned change, involves systematic applications of behavioral science to the planned development and reinforcement of strategies, structures, and processes that lead to organizational effectiveness (Cummings & Worley, 2001, p. 1). Business-oriented projects aim more explicitly than OD at improving a firm's economic performance and its competitive advantage and rely more on techniques drawn from business, engineering, and other technical fields (Beer & Nobria, 2000).

OD projects can be thought of as moving through a series of stages (Kolb & Frohman, 1970; Waclawski & Church, 2002). Projects usually begin with an entry (or scouting) stage, in which clients and consultants get to know one another and consultants gain their first impressions of the client organization (Levinson, 1994). After consultants and clients clarify their expectations for the consultation and formalize them in a contract, the consultant conducts a diagnosis of the current state of the organization and provides feedback to clients on the findings. Thereafter, consultants and clients work together to define objectives for the change project and plan interventions that will promote desired changes. During the action stage, the consultants guide or actually conduct these interventions, sometimes gathering additional diagnostic data and providing additional feedback on the experimental or transitional phases of the change project. Thereafter, clients and consultants evaluate the results of the project. In practice, consultation in OD often shifts back and forth between these stages rather than following them sequentially (e.g., Case 4, below); some projects skip one or more stages (e.g., evaluation).

OD consultants may engage in diagnostic activities during several phases of a consultation. In particular, during entry, consultants may unobtrusively observe interactions between clients and other members of the organization to get a feel for interpersonal processes and power relations. At the same time, consultants may also conduct interviews or discussions with important members to become familiar with the organization and assess members' attitudes toward the proposed consulting project. Consultants will also read available documents on the organization's history, goals, and current operations. Based on this information, consultants usually make a preliminary diagnosis of the organization's needs and strengths and its capacity for improvement and change. In particular, experienced practitioners seek to determine as early as possible whether key members of an organization are likely to cooperate with a more formal and extended diagnosis and whether these people are able to make decisions and act in response to feedback. This preliminary diagnosis can determine the subsequent development of the project. As consultants and clients discuss these preliminary assessments, they redefine their expectations for the consultation. This process increases the chances that the consultation will benefit the clients and helps both parties avoid entering a relationship that will become an exercise in frustration.

Diagnosis itself can be a form of intervention because it interrupts organizational routines, may affect members' expectations concerning change, and may influence how they think about themselves and their organization (Argyris, 1970). In process consultation (Schein, 1998), for example, the practitioner provides diagnostic feedback on group processes to heighten awareness of these processes and thereby help participants improve them. Similarly, practitioners sometimes conduct diagnostic workshops for management teams or steering committees responsible for change projects (e.g., see p. 113). The workshops are intended to promote teamwork and facilitate planning and decision making. During workshops, the consultants may help participants examine their organization's culture, clarify their goals and strategies, or consider ways to restructure the organization.

Traditionally, OD consultants assumed that organizations become more effective as they foster reductions in power and status differences, open communication, participative decision making, cooperation, solidarity, and development of their members' human potential (Strauss, 1976). Moreover, OD practitioners envisioned a broad role for consultants in helping organizations move toward this ideal type of structure and culture. To promote change and development, OD consultants developed a wide range of intervention techniques (Burke, 1993; Cummings & Worley, 2001; Porras & Robertson, 1987). Here is a summary of these interventions, grouped by the part of the organizational system that is most directly targeted:

- *Human resources:* changing or selecting for skills, attitudes, and values through training programs and courses; recruitment, selection, counseling, and placement; and stress management and health-maintenance programs
- *Behavior and processes:* changing interaction processes, such as decision making, leadership, and communication, through training, team building, process consultation, and third-party intervention for conflict resolution; and feedback of survey data for self-diagnosis and action planning
- *Organizational structures and technologies:* redesigning jobs, administrative procedures, reward mechanisms, the division of labor, coordinating mechanisms, and work procedures
- *Organizational goals, strategies, and cultures:* promoting goal clarification and strategy formulation through workshops and exercises; facilitating cooperative ties between organizations; and examining and changing corporate cultures (values, norms, and beliefs)

OD consultants rely on several sources of knowledge as they decide which intervention techniques are likely to produce the desired results. These sources include evidence gathered during diagnosis, the consultants' experience, books and papers by practitioners, behavioral science research on organizations and management, and a growing body of research on organizational change (Beer, Eisenstat, & Spector, 1990; Hackman & Wageman, 1995; Huber & Glick, 1993; Macy & Izumi, 1993; Porras & Robertson, 1992; Porras & Silver, 1991; Weick & Quinn, 1999).

Diagnosis can also make a vital contribution to more technical and business-oriented types of change management. Currently, even managers of not-for-profit organizations pursue financial and business-like objectives as they respond to tight budgets and competition from other organizations. Change management in pursuit of economic objectives is usually driven more by top managers and makes more use of business and technical tools than do OD projects. For example, business process reengineering (BPR) calls for the redesign of major functional areas within an organization so as to enhance the performance of core business processes, such as customer service, order fulfillment, and acquisitions (Hammer & Champy, 1993).

Some change projects seek to combine a focus on economic value with an OD-like concern for developing organizational and human capabilities (Beer & Nobria, 2000). Many current programs in strategic human resource management (Becker, Huselid, & Ulrich, 2001; Jackson & Schuler, 1995; Neill & Mindrum, 2000) contain this dual focus, as do some quality improvement programs.

Change management consultants can use diagnosis to help clients decide what changes in organizational features are likely to promote desired outcomes, how ready members are for these changes, and how managers can best implement changes and ensure their sustainability. Research on downsizing in the automobile industry provides one indication of the potential payoffs of carefully diagnosing the needs and prospects for change and developing interventions that are tailored to prevailing conditions within the focal organization. A 4-year study of downsizing among 30 firms in the automobile industry (Cameron, 1994; Cameron, Freeman, & Mishra, 1991) showed that firms that planned and designed downsizing moves through systematic analyses of jobs, resource usage, work flow, and implications for human resource management were more likely to attain subsequent improvements in performance. Furthermore, these firms were more able to avoid common negative consequences of downsizing, such as loss of valued employees and declining morale among remaining employees.

Unfortunately, many ambitious change projects that could benefit from careful diagnosis do not make much use of it (Harrison, 2004; Harrison & Shirom, 1999). For example, BPR requires a substantial investment on the part of the organization, carries high risks (e.g., disruption of routine practices), and often leads to major personnel reductions. BPR projects have not usually achieved the ambitious objectives anticipated by reengineering's early champions for cost reduction, productivity gains, and faster cycling of core processes (Champy, 1995, p. 3). Nonetheless, during the heyday of BPR, its practitioners paid little attention to diagnosis (Harrison & Shirom, 1999, pp. 178–179). In addition, analyses of BPR failures (Clemons, Thatcher, & Row, 1995; Grey & Mitev, 1995) overlooked the possibility that project failures were partly precipitated by inadequate diagnosis of the organization's needs, its change options, and its capacity for implementing BPR.

Freestanding Diagnostic Studies

In addition to forming a stage in a change project, diagnosis can take the form of an independent consulting project, in which practitioners contract with clients about the nature of the study, design it, gather and analyze data, provide written and oral feedback on their findings, and make recommendations. In these projects, as occurred in Case 2, formal relations between clients and consultants end with the delivery of the diagnostic report.

Consultants and clients often prefer this approach for studies that focus on a specific organizational problem. Freestanding studies are also popular when experts assess a specific set of administrative activities, such as an employee safety program, or when they help design new programs. For example, Case 6 describes how practitioners might assess the degree to which management training programs in a multinational firm build the skills needed for managing operations on a worldwide basis. An assessment study such as this could serve as the basis for developing recommendations for redesigning the firm's management training activities to meet challenges posed by globalization. Even if clients have already decided on a structural or technical design change, such as a new departmental structure or acquisition of new information technology, consultants can use diagnostic techniques to track progress toward implementation and provide early warning of unanticipated effects of the design change (Harrison & Shirom, 1999, chap. 7).

Freestanding diagnostic studies can also facilitate managerial efforts to bring about complex, far-reaching organizational transformations (Bartunek & Louis, 1988; Nadler, Shaw, Walton, & Associates, 1995). Transformations involve fundamental changes in organizational features, such as structures, technologies, goals, strategies, and culture (Kizer, 1999). Transformations usually require members of the organization to bend or break out of accepted ways of thinking and acting and develop new frames for understanding and evaluating their work. Such changes usually evolve over a period of several years under the leadership of top management (Tichy & DeVanna, 1997). Efforts to accomplish transformations often occur after major shifts in power alignments within and outside of the organization or after organizations have undergone crises that threaten their survival. To accomplish fundamental changes, management may draw on the advice of consultants with expertise in many different areas. Diagnostic studies can help management assess the need for transformation and the best ways of accomplishing it. Moreover, consultants can help monitor the effects of managerial actions and other organizational changes as they occur. Similarly, consultants may help managers plan, conduct, and monitor downsizing activities so as to preserve their organization's core competencies (Nutt, 2001).

Self-Diagnosis

Members of an organization can conduct a self-diagnosis without the aid of a professional consultant provided they are open to self-analysis and criticism and some members have the skills needed for data gathering and analysis. Here is an example of a modest self-diagnosis (Austin, 1982, p. 20):

Case 3

The executive director of a multiservice youth agency appointed a program review committee to make a general evaluation of the services provided by the agency and recommend ways to improve service effectiveness. The committee included clinical case workers, supervisors, administrators, and several members of the agency's governing board. The director of the agency, who had the technical knowledge needed to conduct this type of study, served as an adviser to the committee. She asked the committee members to look first at the agency's intake service because it was central to the operations of the entire agency and suffered from high turnover among its paid staff. Besides examining intake operations, the committee members decided to investigate whether clients were getting appropriate services. They interviewed both the paid and the volunteer intake staff and surveyed clients during a 3-month period. Their main finding was that substantial delays occurred in client referral to counseling. They traced these delays to difficulties that the half-time coordinator of intake faced in handling the large staff of paid employees and volunteers; they also linked delays to the heavy burden of record keeping that fell on the intake workers. This paperwork was required by funding agencies but did not contribute directly to providing services to clients. To increase satisfaction among intake staff and thereby reduce turnover, the committee recommended that the coordinator's position be made full-time and paperwork at intake be reduced. The executive director accepted the first recommendation and asked for further study of how to streamline the record-keeping process and reduce paperwork.

As this case suggests, during self-diagnosis, members of the organization temporarily take on some of the tasks that would otherwise be the responsibility of a professional consultant. Many of the diagnostic models and research techniques described in this book and in other guides to diagnosis (Howard & Associates, 1994) could contribute to such self-studies. People who want to conduct a self-diagnosis or act as informal consultants to self-study groups should be skilled at handling the interpersonal relations that develop during a study, giving feedback to groups and individuals, and gathering and analyzing diagnostic data.

Comparisons to Other Types of Organizational Research

Another way of understanding diagnosis is to contrast it to other forms of organizational research. As defined here, diagnosis does not include investigations of programs or entire organizations by external commissions of inquiry or governmental agencies (Gormley & Weimer, 1999). These investigations do not create client-consultant relations of the sort described previously and do not rely mainly on behavioral science methods and models. Nor does diagnosis refer to other forms of assessment and applied research designed to help decision makers assess specific programs and decide on ways to allocate funds (Freeman, Dynes, Rossi, & Whyte, 1983; Harrison & Shirom, 1999; Lusthaus, Adrien, Anderson, Carden, & Montvalvan, 2002; Majchrzak, 1984). These studies usually have a narrower research focus than diagnosis. For example, an applied research study may seek to identify the causes of an outcome of concern, such as alcohol abuse or work accidents.

Diagnosis has more in common with evaluation research (Patton, 1999; Rossi, Freeman, & Lipsey, 1999), in which behavioral science research contributes to the planning, monitoring, and assessment of the costs and impacts of social programs in areas such as health, education, and welfare (e.g., the impact of a standards assessment program on pupils' reading skills). Like diagnosis, evaluation is practically oriented and may focus on effectiveness. Diagnostic studies, however, often examine a broader spectrum of indicators of organizational effectiveness than do summative evaluations, which assess program effects or program efficiency. Diagnostic studies also differ from most formative evaluations, which monitor program implementation. Most diagnostic studies examine a broader range of organizational features, whereas formative evaluations usually concentrate on the extent to which a project was conducted according to plan. An additional difference is that diagnoses are often conducted on much more restricted budgets, within shorter time frames, and must rely on less extensive forms of data gathering and analysis.

Despite these differences, many of the models used in diagnosis can contribute to strategy assessments and program evaluations (Harrison & Shirom,

1999), and diagnostic practitioners can benefit from the extensive literature on evaluation techniques and processes. Practitioners of diagnosis can also incorporate concepts and methods from strategic assessments of intraorganizational factors shaping performance and strategic advantage (Duncan, Ginter, & Swayne, 1998; Kaplan & Norton, 1996).

Diagnosis differs substantially from nonapplied, academic research on organizations in its emphasis on obtaining results that will be immediately useful to members of a client organization (Block, 2000). Unlike academic researchers, practitioners of diagnosis

- concentrate on finding readily changeable factors that affect an organizational problem or condition, even if these factors do not explain most of the variance and are not the most important or interesting from a researcher's point of view;

- may encourage the members of the organization under study to become involved in the research;

- may use less complex research designs and methods (e.g., simpler sampling procedures, a few open-ended observational categories instead of many precoded ones, and fewer control variables);

- need to rely more on hunches, experience, and intuition as well as on scientific methods when gathering and analyzing data and formulating conclusions and recommendations;

- cannot remain neutral about the impact of their study on the organization and the needs and concerns of members of the organization.

THREE KEYS TO SUCCESSFUL DIAGNOSIS

Diagnosis can succeed only if it provides its clients with data, analyses, and recommendations that are useful and valid. To meet these dual standards, the diagnostic practitioner must fill the requirements of three key facets of diagnosis—process, modeling, and methods—and needs to ensure good alignments among all three.

Process

The texture of client-consultant relations poses clear requirements for successful diagnosis: To provide genuinely useful findings and recommendations, consultants need to create and maintain cooperative, constructive relations with clients. Moreover, to ensure that their study yields valid and useful results, practitioners of diagnosis must successfully negotiate their relations with other members of the focal organization during all phases of the diagnosis.

Phases in Diagnosis

Diagnostic studies typically include several distinct phases (Nadler, 1977). As the following description shows, diagnostic tasks, models, and methods shift within and between phases, as do relations between consultants, clients, and other members of the client organization:

- *Entry:* Clients and consultants explore expectations for the study; the client presents problems and challenges; the consultant assesses the likelihood of cooperation with various types of research and probable receptiveness to feedback; and the consultant makes a preliminary reconnaissance of organizational problems and strengths.

- *Contracting:* Consultants and clients negotiate and agree on the nature of the diagnosis and client-consultant relations.

- *Study design:* Methods, measurement procedures, sampling, analysis, and administrative procedures are planned.

- *Data gathering:* Data are gathered through interviews, observations, questionnaires, analysis of secondary data, group discussions, and workshops.

- *Analysis:* Consultants analyze the data and summarize findings; consultants (and sometimes clients) interpret them and prepare for feedback.

- *Feedback:* Consultants present findings to clients and other members of the client organization; feedback may include explicit recommendations or more general findings to stimulate discussion, decision making, and action planning.

As Case 4 suggests, these phases can overlap in practice, and their sequence may vary.

Case 4

The owner and chief executive officer (CEO) of 21C, a small high-technology firm, asked a private consultant to examine ways to improve efficiency and morale in the firm. They agreed that staff from the consulting firm would conduct a set of in-depth interviews with divisional managers and a sample of other employees. The first interviews with the three division heads and the assistant director suggested that their frustrations and poor morale stemmed from the firm's lack of growth and the CEO's failure to include the managers in decision making and strategy formulation. In light of these findings, the consultant returned to the CEO, discussed the results of the interviews, and suggested refocusing the diagnosis on relations between the managers and the CEO and the firm's processes for planning and strategy formation.

In the 21C project, analysis, and feedback began before completion of data gathering. Moreover, the diagnosis shifted back into the contracting phase in the midst of data gathering, when the consultant sought approval to redefine the diagnostic problem and change the research design.

Critical Process Issues

The relations that develop between practitioners and members of a client organization can greatly affect the outcomes of an organizational diagnosis, just as they affect other aspects of consulting (Block, 2000; Turner, 1982). Although clients and practitioners should try to define their expectations early in the project, they will often need to redefine their relations during the course of the diagnosis to deal with issues that were neglected during initial contracting or arose subsequently. To manage the consulting relation successfully, practitioners need to handle the following key process issues (Nadler, 1977; Van de Ven & Ferry, 1980, pp. 22-51) in ways that promote cooperation between themselves and members of the client organization:

- *Purpose:* What are the goals of the study, how are they defined, and how can the outcomes of the study be evaluated? What issues, challenges, and problems are to be studied?

- *Design:* How will members of the organization be affected by the study design and methods (e.g., organizational features to be studied, units and individuals included in data gathering, and types of data-collection techniques)?

- *Support and cooperation:* Who sponsors and supports the study, and what resources will the client organization contribute? What are the attitudes of other members of the organization and of external stakeholders toward the study?

- *Participation:* What role will members of the organization play in planning the study and gathering, interpreting, and reacting to the data?

- *Feedback:* When, how, and in what format will feedback be given? Who will receive feedback on the study, and what uses will they make of the data?

As these questions suggest, clients and consultants must make difficult and consequential decisions concerning participation in the study by members of the focal organization. Freestanding diagnostic studies are usually consultant centered because the consultant accepts sole or primary responsibility for conducting all phases of the diagnosis. After the clients approve the proposed study, they and other members of the organization may not take an active role in it until they receive feedback on the findings. Practitioners often prefer this type of diagnosis because it seems simpler and more suitable to objective, rigorous research. Clients too often prefer to limit their investment in diagnosis and wait for the results of the study before committing to additional interventions.

A frequent result of this separation of diagnosis from action is that clients do not act on the consultant's recommendations because they view them as irrelevant or unworkable (Block, 2000; Turner, 1982). Skillful consultants may partially overcome this problem by meeting periodically with clients to provide interim feedback and encouraging clients to evaluate the feedback and consider its implications for action. In this manner, consultants increase the chances that their findings will reflect the experiences and perceptions of key clients and will therefore be believable to clients. Moreover, periodic discussions of the study may encourage clients to feel more responsibility for diagnostic findings and recommendations.

In contrast to consultant-centered studies, diagnosis within OD projects is often highly client centered—in the sense of involving clients or members appointed by them in as many phases of diagnosis as is feasible (Lawler & Drexler, 1980; Turner, 1982). This approach encourages members of the client organization to contribute their insights and expertise as they share in data gathering and analysis. Participation in diagnosis often enhances the credibility and salience of diagnostic findings. In addition, involvement in diagnosis may help members develop the capacity to assess their own operations. This capacity for routine self-assessment can help members develop the ability to cope continually with social, technological, and economic changes.

Despite these advantages, client-centered diagnosis has serious limitations and drawbacks. First, it is likely to have the sought-after effects only when the culture of the client organization supports open communication, respect for divergent viewpoints, and honest confrontation of organizational and individual limitations. Many national and organizational cultures do not value these conditions highly. Moreover, these conditions are typically lacking in organizations undergoing decline or divided by serious conflicts. Second, client-centered diagnoses may fail to yield valid conclusions because participants are biased in favor of a particular diagnosis and set of action recommendations. In other instances, participants may lack the data and skills needed to identify forces that are producing symptoms of ineffectiveness or other system problems. Third, client-centered diagnosis works best in face-to-face problem-solving groups. To participate successfully in such groups, participants require prior training or experience in teamwork. Moreover, participants in diagnostic teams need to be empowered to act on their findings. These requirements usually restrict the application of client-centered approaches to top managers or heads of semiautonomous units. Fourth, client-centered diagnoses may actually reduce the prospects for organizational change by giving opponents of change additional opportunities to delay or divert steps toward change.

Modeling

The success of a diagnosis depends greatly on the ways that practitioners handle the analytic tasks of framing and defining diagnostic problems, analyzing results, and providing feedback.[4] Behavioral science models and the broader orienting metaphors (Morgan, 1996) and frames (Bolman & Deal, 2003) from which models derive can help practitioners decide what to study, choose measures of organizational effectiveness, and identify conditions that promote or block effectiveness.

Models

Many practitioners use models developed by experienced consultants and applied researchers to guide their investigations (for reviews, see Appendix B; Faletta & Combs, 2002; Harrison & Shirom, 1999; Howard & Associates, 1994). These models specify organizational features that have proved critical in the past. Standardized models also help large consulting practices maintain consistency across projects. Unfortunately, work with available models runs the risks of generating much data that are difficult to interpret, failing to address challenges and problems that are critical to clients, and not reflecting distinctive features of the client organization. To avoid these drawbacks, consultants often tailor standardized models to fit the client organization and its circumstances (Burke, Coruzzi, & Church, 1996).

Another way of addressing these issues is to develop grounded models that emerge during initial study of the organization and focus more directly on client concerns. For example, in "sharp-image diagnosis" (Harrison & Shirom, 1999), the practitioner uses one or more theoretical frames as orienting devices and then develops a model that specifies the forces affecting the problems or challenges presented by clients. This model also guides feedback. In the CHF case (Case 2), the diagnosis drew on two frames. The first applied open systems concepts to the analysis of strategic organizational change (Tichy, 1983). This frame guided analysis of the capacity of CHF's proposed strategy to revitalize the organization and help it cope with external challenges. Second, a political frame guided analysis of the ability of CHF's director to mobilize support for the proposed transformation and overcome opposition among staff members. For feedback, elements from both frames were combined into a single model that directed attention to findings and issues of greatest importance for action planning.

As they examine diagnostic issues and data, practitioners often frame issues differently than clients do. The director of CHF originally defined the problem as one of resistance to change, whereas the HMO's director of training phrased the original diagnostic problem in terms of assessing the need for the training program. The consultant reframed the study task by dividing it in two: assessing feasibility of accomplishing the proposed organizational transformation and discovering steps that CHF management and the HMO could take to facilitate the transformation. This redefinition of the diagnostic task thus included an image of the organization's desired state that fit both client expectations and social science knowledge about organizational effectiveness. Moreover, this reformulation helped specify the issues that should be studied in-depth and suggested ways that the clients could deal with the problems that initially concerned them. The consultant's recommendations took into account which possible solutions to problems were more likely to be accepted and could be successfully implemented by the clients.

Diagnostic Questions

The following set of diagnostic questions capture critical analytical themes facing consultants and highlight the ways that consultants frame issues and conditions that are presented to them:[5]

1. *Interpreting the initial statement of the problem:*[6] How does the client initially define the problems, needs, and challenges facing the organization or unit? How does the client view the desired state of the organization?

2. *Redefining the problem:* How can the problem be redefined so it can be investigated and workable solutions can be developed? What will be the focal points of the diagnosis? What assumptions about the preferred state of the organization and definitions of organizational effectiveness will be used in the diagnosis? How will solving the problem improve effectiveness?

3. *Understanding the current state:* What individuals, groups, and components of the organization are most affected by this redefined problem and most likely to be involved in or affected by its solution? How is the problem currently being dealt with? How do members of the relevant groups define the problem and suggest solving it?

4. *Identifying forces for and against change:* What internal and external groups and conditions create pressure for organizational change, and what are the sources of resistance to it? How ready and capable of changing are the people and groups who are most affected by the problem and its possible solutions? Do they have common interests or needs that could become a basis for working together to solve the problem?

5. *Developing workable solutions:* Which behavior patterns and organizational arrangements can be most easily changed to solve problems and improve effectiveness? What interventions are most likely to produce these desired outcomes?

To increase the chances that clients will understand, accept, and act on feedback, successful consultants try to remain aware of gaps between their own analyses and members' interpretations. Moreover, practitioners challenge client views only in areas that are crucial to organizational improvement.

Level of Analysis

A major interpretive issue facing consultants concerns the level of analysis at which they will examine a problem and suggest dealing with it. Questions about people's attitudes, motivations, and work behavior focus on the individual level. Those dealing with face-to-face relations are at the interpersonal level. At the group level are questions about the performance and practices of departments or work units, such as those raised in Case 3. Next are questions at the divisional level about the management of major subunits (divisions, branches, and factories) within large organizations and about relations among units within divisions. Some investigations, such as the study of CHF, examine the organization as a whole and its relations to its environment. Finally, diagnosis sometimes examines a network of interacting organizations or an entire sector or industry, such as the health-care sector (Harrison & Shirom, 1999, chap. 14).

Many important phenomena show up at more than one level of analysis. In a manufacturing division, for example, the main technology (work tools and techniques) might be computer-aided manufacturing, which uses robots and flexible manufacturing systems (Sussman, 1990). At the group level, each work group would have its own techniques and equipment for monitoring the highly automated operations. At the individual level are specific equipment and control procedures at each work station. Certain other phenomena can best be observed at one particular level. For instance, the speed with which the firm decides to make new products, develops them, and brings them to market can best be examined at the level of the total organization.

The choice of levels of analysis in diagnosis should reflect the nature of the problem, the goals of the diagnosis, and the organizational location of clients. In choosing levels of analysis, consultants need to consider whether higher-level phenomena support or block change in lower-level ones. Hospital payment systems, for example, may not provide sufficient incentives and may even create disincentives for organizational-level quality improvement (Ferlie & Shortell, 2001). To facilitate diagnosis and increase the chances that clients will implement recommendations, practitioners usually concentrate on organizational features over which their clients have considerable control. Changes in the departmental structure of an entire division, for example, can occur only with the support of top management. Furthermore, diagnosis is more useful when it examines levels at which interventions are most likely to lead to organizational improvement. Suppose, for example, that managers asked for a diagnosis of problems related to employee performance. Consultants would examine the rules and procedures for monitoring, controlling, and rewarding performance if these design tools could be readily changed by managerial clients. Other influential factors, such as workers' informal relations and their work norms and values, might not be examined in detail because they would be more difficult to change.

By changing the level of analysis, consultants and clients can sometimes discover relations and possibilities for change that were not previously apparent (Rashford & Coghlan, 1994). For instance, rather than concentrating exclusively on administrator-subordinate relations within an underproductive department in a public agency, consultants might examine the group's location within the work flow of the entire division. This shift in level of analysis might point to coordination problems within the division as a whole that must be solved before work group productivity can be improved.

Scope

Practitioners must also decide on the scope of their study. An individual-level diagnosis of broad scope would try to take into account the major factors related to the performance and feelings of the people within a focal unit (see Chapter 3). In contrast, a more narrowly focused diagnosis in the same unit and at the same level of analysis might examine only factors related to job satisfaction. Studies with a broad scope may uncover sources of problems or potential solutions that were not evident to clients and consultants at the start of the diagnosis. Consultants conducting broad studies, however, risk spending much time gathering and analyzing data that are not useable or directly relevant to client concerns. Instead, by focusing directly on the forces underlying problems and challenges presented by clients, consultants can provide more rapid feedback and more useful and actionable findings (Harrison & Shirom, 1999).

In summary, models and analytical frames based on current research can serve as guides to diagnosis, but they cannot tell practitioners in advance exactly what to study, how to interpret diagnostic data, or what interventions will work best in a particular client organization. Research shows that managerial practices and organizational patterns that promote effectiveness in one type of organization (e.g., new family businesses) will not necessarily contribute to effectiveness in another organization faced with different conditions (e.g., mature, professionally managed firms). The chapters that follow note some of the important conditions or contingencies that help determine which facets of organizational effectiveness are most important and which managerial practices and organizational forms contribute most to effectiveness.[7]

Methods

Successful diagnosis also requires methods that ensure valid findings and contribute to constructive relations between consultants and members of the client organization.

Choosing Methods

To provide valid results, practitioners should employ the most rigorous methods possible within the practical constraints imposed by the nature of the assignment. Rigorous methods—which need not be quantitative—follow accepted standards of scientific inquiry (King, Keohane, & Verba, 1994). They have a high probability of producing results that are valid and reliable (i.e., replicable by other trained investigators) (Trochim, 2001). Nonrigorous approaches can yield valid results, but these cannot be externally evaluated or replicated. In assessing the validity of their diagnoses, practitioners need to be aware of the risk of false-positive results that might lead them to recommend steps that are unjustified and even harmful to the client organization (Rossi & Whyte, 1983).

To achieve replicability, practitioners can use structured data-gathering and measurement techniques, such as fixed-choice questionnaires or observations using a standard coding scheme. Unfortunately, it is very difficult to structure techniques for assessing many complex but important phenomena, such as the degree to which managers accurately interpret environmental developments.

To produce valid and reliable results, investigators often must sort out conflicting opinions and perspectives about the organization and construct an independent assessment. The quest for an independent viewpoint and scientific rigor should not, however, prevent investigators from treating the plurality of interests and perspectives within a focal organization as a significant organizational feature in its own right (Hennestad, 1988; Ramirez & Bartunek, 1989).

Whatever techniques practitioners use in diagnosis, it is best to avoid methodological overkill when only a rough estimate of the extent of a particular phenomenon is needed. In Case 4, for example, the investigators needed to determine whether division heads were frustrated and dissatisfied and to find the sources of the managers' feelings. The practitioners did not need to specify the precise degree of managerial dissatisfaction, as they might have done in an academic research study.

Consultants need to consider the implications of their methods for the consulting process and the analytic issues at hand, as well as weighing strictly practical and methodological considerations. Thus, consultants might prefer to use less rigorous methods, such as discussions of organizational conditions in workshop settings, because these methods can enhance the commitment of participants to the diagnostic study and its findings. Also, they might prefer observations to interviews so as not to encourage people to expect that the consultation would address the many concerns that might be raised during interviews.

The methods chosen and the ways that data are presented to clients also need to fit the culture of the client organization. In a high-technology firm, for example, people may regard qualitative research as impressionistic and unscientific. Volunteers at a hospice, however, might view standardized questionnaires and quantitative analysis as insensitive to their feelings and experiences.

Research Design

Three types of nonexperimental designs seem most appropriate for diagnosis. The first involves gathering data on important criteria that allow for comparisons between units or between entire organizations (e.g., Case 1). Comparisons may focus on criteria such as client satisfaction, organizational climate (e.g., perceptions of peer and subordinate-supervisor relations and identification with unit and organizational goals), personnel turnover, costs, and sales. Sometimes, practitioners can analyze available records or make repeated measurements to trace changes in key variables across time for each unit or for an entire set of related units.

The second design uses multivariate analysis of data to isolate the causes or predictors of variables linked to a particular organizational problem, such as work quality or employee turnover, or to some desirable outcome, such as product innovation or customer satisfaction. The third design uses qualitative field techniques to construct a portrait of the operations of a small organization or subunit and obtain in-depth data on subtle, difficult to measure features that may be lost or distorted in close-ended inquiries. Among such features are members' perceptions, hidden assumptions, behind-the-scenes interactions, and work styles (see Chapter 4). In such qualitative studies, investigators use data-gathering techniques and inductive forms of inference such as those used in nonapplied qualitative research (Denzin & Lincoln, 2000; Dougherty, 2002; Miles & Huberman, 1994; Van de Ven & Poole, 2002; Yin, 2002). To ensure quick feedback, however, diagnostic studies usually seek less ethnographic detail than nonapplied qualitative research and use less rigorous forms of recording and analyzing field data.

Data Collection

Table 1.1 surveys and assesses data-collection techniques frequently used in diagnosis. Additional details on these techniques appear in the chapters that follow, texts on research methods (Miller & Salkind, 2002; Trochim, 2001), the references to the table, and Appendixes A, B, and C. No single method for gathering and analyzing data can suit every diagnostic problem and situation, just as there is no universal model for guiding diagnostic analysis or one ideal procedure for managing the diagnostic process. By using several methods to gather and analyze data, practitioners can compensate for many of the drawbacks associated with relying on a single method (Jick, 1979). They also need to choose methods that fit the diagnostic problems and contribute to cooperative, productive consulting relations.

Table 1.1
Comparison of Methods for Gathering Diagnostic Data*

Method	Advantages	Disadvantages
Questionnaires		
Self-administered schedules, fixed choices (Chapter 3 and Appendix B, this volume; Church & Waclawski, 1998; Faletta & Combs, 2002; Kraut, 1996)	Easy to quantify and summarize; quickest and cheapest way to gather new data rigorously, neutral and objective; useful for large samples, repeat measures, and comparisons among units or to norms; standardized instruments contain pretested items, reflect diagnostic models, and are good for studying attitudes	Difficult-to-obtain data on structure and behavior; little information on how contexts shape behavior; not suited for subtle or sensitive issues; impersonal; risks: nonresponse, biased or invalid answers, and overreliance on standard measures and models
Interviews Open-ended questions based on fixed schedule or interview guide (Chapters 2, 3, and 5 and Appendix A, this volume; Greenbaum, 1998; McCracken, 1988; Waclawski & Rogelberg, 2002)	Can cover many topics; modifiable before or during interview; can convey empathy, build trust; rich data, allows understanding of respondents' viewpoints and perceptions	Expensive and difficult to administer to large samples; respondent bias and socially desirable responses; noncomparable responses; difficult to analyze responses to open-ended questions; modification of interviews to fit respondents reduces rigor
Observations Structured or open-ended observation of people and work settings (Chapters 2 and 3 and Appendix C, this volume; Lofland & Lofland, 1995; Weick, 1985)	Data independent of people's self-presentation and biases; data on situational, contextual effects; rich data on difficult-to-measure topics (e.g., emergent behavior and culture); data yield new insights and hypotheses	Constraints on access to data; costly and time-consuming; observer bias and low reliability; may affect behavior of those observed; difficult to analyze and report; less rigorous, may seem unscientific
Available Records and Data Use of documents, reports, files, statistical records, unobtrusive measures (Chapters 2 and 5, this volume; Kinnear & Taylor,	Nonreactive; often quantifiable; repeated measures show change; organization's members can help analyze data; credibility of familiar	Access, retrieval, analysis problems can raise costs; validity, credibility of some sources and derived measures can be low; need to analyze data

(Continued)

Table 1.1 (Continued)

Method	Advantages	Disadvantages
1987, pp. 152–163, 177–188; Nuendorf, 2002; Stewart, 1992)	measures (e.g., customer complaints, staff turnover); often cheaper and faster than gathering new data; independent sources; data on total organization, environments, industries	data in context; limited information on many topics (e.g., emergent behavior)
Workshops, Group Discussions		
Discussions on group processes, culture, environment, challenges, strategy; directed by consultant or manager; simulations, exercises (Chapter 5, this volume; Biech, 2004; Schein, 1998)	Useful data on complex, subtle process; interaction stimulates creativity, teamwork, planning; data available for immediate analysis and feedback; members share in diagnosis; self-diagnosis possible; consultant can build trust and empathy	Biases due to group processes, history, and leader's influence (e.g., boss stifles dissent); requires high levels of trust and cooperation in group; impressionistic and nonrigorous; may yield superficial, biased results and unsubstantiated decisions

*SOURCES: Earlier versions of this table derived in part from Bowditch and Buono (1989, pp. 32–33), Nadler (1977, p. 119), and Sutherland (1978, p. 163).

DIAGNOSIS IN TURBULENT TIMES

Managers today operate in uncertain economic and political environments. Globalization, shifting alliances among firms, intense competition, and customization of products and services place a premium on responding quickly to market forces. Managers of not-for-profits face tight budgets, along with growing demands for accountability and responsiveness to client concerns. Information technologies are gradually changing the way people organize businesses, do their work, communicate, and spend their leisure time (O'Mahoney & Barley, 1999), and the pace of technological change seems to be increasing.

Is it reasonable to expect managers and other decision makers (e.g., board members, government administrators, and leaders) to engage in systematic diagnosis and decision making when they face such unfamiliar and rapidly changing situations? Does it make sense to plan systematically for organizational changes that will rapidly become outmoded? When external turbulence reaches a state of "permanent white water" (Vaill, 1989), can decisions about organizational change still proceed through the classic sequence of diagnosis, planning, action, and evaluation?

The answer to these questions is that the very conditions that create barriers to diagnosis and systematic decision making also render them essential. Diagnosis can help managers avoid two types of risky response to uncertainty—avoiding change and acting inappropriately. Managers in organizations that have performed well in the past often become resistant to change. Past attainments create a "success trap" by reinforcing the incorrect and ultimately dangerous assumption that the best way to handle future challenges is to rely on strategies and tactics that worked well in the past (Nadler & Shaw, 1995). Managers facing external threats and declining revenues may also avoid change just when the need to move in new directions is greatest (McKinley, 1993). Diagnosis can make the risks of inaction evident to managers in both situations and can help them choose more appropriate responses to their environment.

The other possibility, which also carries great risks, is that as external conditions worsen, managers will act blindly without carefully analyzing the likely effects of their decisions (Weitzel & Jonsson, 1989). These unsystematic actions have low chances of success and can actually weaken an organization's capacity for recovery. Even managers in successful organizations need to be cautious about action that is not grounded in careful analysis. Uncritical imitation of fashionable practices, which offer quick fixes to fundamental problems, can waste resources and delay effective actions (Abrahamson, 1996; Abrahamson & Fairchild, 1999; Harrison, 2004). Diagnosis can help managers decide whether popular techniques and new organization designs are likely to help them meet the challenges at hand. If the techniques seem appropriate, managers and consultants can plan action steps and follow-up that will help them learn from experience and avoid the pitfalls that often accompany the unsystematic implementation of new structures and management practices.

When managers face rapidly changing and uncertain conditions, they need to act quickly and flexibly—diagnosing their situation, developing strategies, planning actions, and initiating them. Moreover, they need to constantly track environmental and internal changes and assess the results of their actions. Then, they can modify their actions or shift course altogether. Rather than relying on elaborate decision processes and time-consuming strategic planning programs, decision makers facing dynamic and turbulent conditions must move through this type of diagnostic inquiry quickly and experimentally— continually formulating, checking, and reformulating their interpretations and explanations (Schon, 1983). Frequent feedback on previous actions provides the basis for this learning process. When feedback or additional data fail to support managers' expectations about the environment and about their own organization, or when new opportunities arise, the managers can reassess their guiding strategy and rediagnose their operations (Huber & Glick, 1993; Pascale, 1984; Quinn, 1980).

CONCLUSION AND PLAN OF THE BOOK

This chapter located diagnosis within organization development and more business-oriented change management projects and presented methodological, analytic, and processual issues that affect the success of diagnostic consultations. To link this introductory chapter with the ones that follow, several generalizations, which inform the presentation of diagnosis throughout this book, are presented here. First, organizations can best be examined as open systems in which there are interactions between organizations and their environments and among internal system components (human and material resources, structures, technologies, processes, and culture). Gradually, system components become aligned with one another. Incremental (small-scale and gradual) changes can take place without disturbing prevailing system features and connections among them; radical change, however, requires realignments of major system features (Romanelli & Tushman, 1994). Second, the people and groups who influence organizational decisions often pursue divergent interests and develop divergent views of how the organization operates and what is best for it. As a result, political processes play a crucial role in organizational consultation and change (Greiner & Schein, 1988; Harrison, 1991; Harrison & Shirom, 1999). Third, consultants can facilitate major organizational changes and transformations, but managers typically drive them (Kilmann, Covin, & Associates, 1988; Tichy & DeVanna, 1997). Fourth, consultants enhance an organization's capacity to deal with future challenges when they help clients develop their own ability to diagnose and act on problems and facilitate development of structures and processes capable of sustaining organizational learning (Argyris & Schon, 1995; Block, 2000).

Chapter 2 shows practitioners how to use open systems models, along with an understanding of organizations as political arenas, to attain an overview of the functioning of a client organization, choose topics for further diagnosis, assess organizational effectiveness, and decide what steps will help clients solve problems and enhance effectiveness. Chapters 3 through 5 present diagnoses of individual and group behavior, fit among system features, organizational politics, and organization design conditions. Emphasis is placed on understanding emergent practices and assessing how organizations deal with environmental constraints and challenges. Exercises for students and practitioners-in-training appear at the end of Chapters 1 through 5. Chapter 6 treats ethical and professional dilemmas confronting practitioners. The appendixes give more details on diagnostic instruments and provide resources for readers seeking to develop background and skills in diagnosis and consultation. The summaries at the beginning of each chapter provide a more detailed view of the book's contents.

EXERCISE

You will probably find it easier and more satisfying to base all the exercises in this book on the same organization. Consider studying an organization in which someone you know can help you gain access to information and influential members. After you have located an organization or unit (e.g., department and branch), discuss the possibility of studying it with a person who could give you permission to do so and could help you learn about the organization. Explain that you want to do several exercises designed to help you learn how consultants and researchers help organizations deal with issues and challenges confronting them and contribute to organizational effectiveness. Promise not to identify the organization, and explain that your reports will be read only by your instructor.

If your contact expresses interest in becoming a client—in the sense of wanting to get feedback from your project—explain that you will be glad to provide oral feedback to the contact person only, provided that the anonymity of the people studied can be preserved. During these discussions, try to learn as much about your contact person's job, views of organizational affairs, degree of interest in your project, and capacity to help with your project. Ask for a tour of the organization's headquarters or physical plant and an overview of the organization's operations.

Next, imagine that you are going to conduct an organizational diagnosis. What have you learned during the entry period that relates to items 1, 2, and 3 in the Diagnostic Questions listed previously in this chapter. Pay particular attention to the way your contact person defined the organization's problems and challenges (threats and opportunities), along with its strengths and weaknesses (see also Exercise 3 in Chapter 5). Do any alternative ways of framing problems and challenges occur to you? Summarize your preliminary experiences and understandings in a report on the following topics:

- Description of the organization and the contact person (including source of access to them)
- Initial contacts, including your feelings and behavior and those of the contact person
- Your contact person's view of the organization's strengths, weaknesses, current problems, challenges, and desired state

- Your understanding of these issues
- Preliminary thoughts about conducting a diagnosis—topics, methods, individuals, and groups to be included

NOTES

1. Models focus on a limited number of concepts and relations among them and may specify variables that operationalize concepts.

2. Unless otherwise noted, the cases are based on my own experiences or those of my colleagues.

3. For the sake of brevity, I often use the term *effectiveness* to include ineffectiveness. Nonetheless, the two phenomena are not strictly comparable. For example, reducing a specific form of ineffectiveness (e.g., production errors) may or may not contribute much to improving a particular measure of effectiveness, such as productivity.

4. *Framing* refers to the ways that theories shape analysis (Bolman & Deal, 2003; Schon & Rein, 1994).

5. The questions are based partly on Beckhard (1969, p. 46) and Block (1981, p. 143).

6. "Problem" refers here to any kind of gap between actual and ideal conditions, including challenges to enter new fields and raise performance standards.

7. Extended treatments of these issues appear in Harrison and Shirom (1999) and in texts on organization design (Daft, 2004) and organizational behavior (Gordon, 2002).

2

Open Systems Models

Models that treat organizations as open systems, along with a view of organizations as political arenas, can help practitioners choose topics for diagnosis, develop criteria for assessing organizational effectiveness, gather data, prepare feedback, and decide what steps, if any, will help clients solve problems and enhance effectiveness. A list of basic organizational information to gather at the start of a diagnosis is provided in this chapter, and methods are discussed for gathering and analyzing data in both broad and focused diagnoses.

USING THE OPEN SYSTEMS APPROACH

The open systems (OS) approach gave rise to a general model that can guide the diagnosis of entire institutional sectors, sets of organizations, individual organizations, divisions, or units within organizations (Cummings & Worley, 2001; Harrison & Shirom, 1999; Katz & Kahn, 1978; Nadler & Tushman, 1989; Senge, 1990). Figure 2.1 presents a useful version of the OS framework.

System Components

The following listing describes the main system components shown in the figure, along with some of their most important subcomponents, and some key aspects of system dynamics:

Inputs (resources) are raw materials, money, people (human resources), equipment, information, knowledge, and legal authorizations that an organization obtains from its environment and that contribute to the creation of its outputs.

Outputs are products, services, and ideas that are the outcomes of organizational action. An organization transfers its main outputs back to the environment and uses others internally. Productivity and performance measures examine the quantity and occasionally the quality of outputs. Human outcomes, which are by-products of system functioning, include behavior such as absenteeism, work effort and cooperation, industrial disputes, turnover, and employee health and safety. In addition, there are subjective outcomes, such as employee satisfaction and perceived quality of working life.

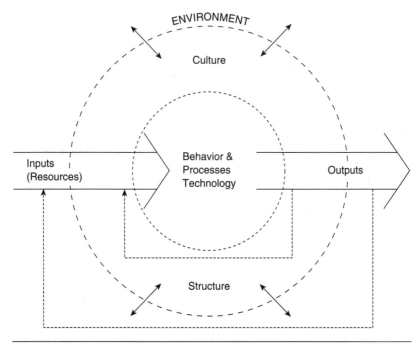

Figure 2.1   Organizations as Open Systems

Key: Broken lines show system boundary. Dotted lines shows feedback loop.

Organizational behavior and processes include prevailing patterns of interaction between individuals and groups, which may contribute directly or indirectly to transforming inputs into outputs. In manufacturing, these transformations are physical. In service organizations such as hospitals, transformative processes include applications of tangible technologies, such as medications, along with mental procedures, such as medical diagnosis, and social procedures, such as patient education. Subcomponents of behavior and processes that are particularly important for handling functional challenges include cooperation, conflict, coordination, communication, controlling and rewarding behavior, influence processes and power relations, supervision, leadership, decision making, problem solving, information gathering, self-criticism, evaluation, group learning, and goal setting. Members' goals and objectives often refer to their expectations for current system performance or for desired future states of inputs, processes, outputs, and other components.

Technology refers to the tools, equipment, and techniques used to process inputs and transform them into outputs.

Environment: The *close (task) environment* includes external organizations and conditions that are directly related to the system's transformative processes and its technologies. The task environment encompasses funding sources, suppliers, distributors, unions, customers, clients, regulators, competitors, strategic partners (e.g., in joint manufacturing ventures), markets for products and resources, and the state of knowledge concerning the organization's technologies. The *remote (general) environment* includes institutions and conditions having infrequent or long-term effects on the organization and its close environment, including the economy, the legal and political systems, the state of scientific and technical knowledge, social institutions such as the family, population distribution and composition, and local or national cultures within which the organization operates.

Structure refers to enduring relations between individuals, groups, and larger units, including role assignments (job descriptions—authority, responsibility, and privileges attached to positions); grouping of positions in divisions, departments, and other units; standard operating procedures; established administrative arrangements for handling key processes, such as coordination (e.g., committees and weekly meetings); control, human resources management, rewards, and planning; job designs; and physical arrangements. Emergent structural patterns (e.g., informal cliques, coalitions, and power distribution) can differ substantially from officially mandated ones. Structure constrains and focuses behavior without determining it.

Culture refers to shared norms, values, beliefs, and assumptions and the behavior and artifacts that express these orientations, including symbols, rituals, stories, and language. Culture includes norms and understandings about the nature and identity of the organization, the way work is done, the value and possibility of changing or innovating, relations between lower and higher ranking members, and the nature of the environment.

System dynamics: The system framework shown in Figure 2.1 contains dynamic features, including feedback of information and demands from within the organization and outside it. Feedback loops appear as dotted lines in Figure 2.1. Important system dynamics that are not depicted in the figure include growth, contraction, development, adjustment, innovation, learning, and changes in basic configurations of system components and subcomponents.

Key Features of the Model

The model implies several important ideas for diagnosis:

1. *The OS frame can be applied at several levels of analysis* (see Chapter 1). Viewing units located at a particular level as systems facilitates diagnostic comparisons among them. Examining interchanges between levels shows that conditions, processes, and outcomes at any given level are often influenced by those at higher and lower levels (Rousseau, 1985). When the systems model is applied to an organization or a unit, such as a project team, that is nested within a larger organization, other units within the organization will constitute much or all of the focal unit's task environment.

2. *Any organizational system may be described as being composed of interdependent components* such as those shown in Figure 2.1. The organization can also be viewed as consisting of subsystems whose functions are delineated in abstract terms, such as maintenance and adaptation, or more concretely in terms of functions, such as human resource management and research and development. Developments within one component within these systems and subsystems can have consequences for other components.

3. *When there is poor fit among interdependent components or functions, effectiveness suffers and signs of ineffectiveness appear* (Harrison & Shirom, 1999). Good fit (or alignment) means that system components or functions reinforce one another rather than disrupting one another's operations (Thompson, 1967, pp. 147–148). Organizational units, system components, or functions fit poorly if their activities erode or cancel each other; if exchanges between units or components lead to avoidable losses of time, money, or energy; or if exchanges and links between units harm their performance.

4. *An organization's effectiveness and success depend heavily on its ability to adapt to its environment, shape that environment, or find a favorable environment in which to operate.* Organization-environment relations form a major focus for OS-guided diagnosis and consultation. External conditions influence resource flows and the reception of outputs. External forces can also directly affect work processes, structure, and other internal system features—for instance, when regulatory agencies define standards for safety, packaging, or advertising. Figure 2.1 depicts the possibility for direct impacts on internal operations by showing a broken, permeable boundary around the organization. In addition to assessing adaptation to external constraints, diagnosis can examine the ways that members of an organization shape their environment. For example, they may form alliances with other organizations or influence the behavior of clients, customers, and regulators.

5. *Organizations use many of their products, services, and ideas as inputs to organizational maintenance or growth.* An information technology firm uses its own software, and a university employs some of its doctoral students as instructors. Individual and group outcomes also feed back into the organization.

6. *People are a vital system resource.* They bring skills, knowledge, experience, and energy to the organization and continue to develop and change after joining it. The background, orientations, and accumulating experience of members influence emergent forms of organizational behavior and culture.

7. *An organization's effectiveness depends substantially on its ability to meet internal system needs—including tying people into their roles in the organization, conducting transformative processes, and managing operations—as well*

as on adaptation to the environment. These "system needs" do not necessarily correspond to the interests or priorities of top management. The nature and intensity of these system requirements vary across the organizational life cycle.

8. *Developments in and outside of organizations produce pressures for change as well as releasing forces for inertia and stability.* Employee behavior and interpretations can reinforce or alter current practices. Change can result from visible pressure (e.g., community protest) and from hidden bargains and alliances. Change can also occur almost imperceptibly as people reinterpret and renegotiate their jobs and their work environments. Change that occurs in response to internal or external problems and pressures is *reactive,* whereas *anticipatory (proactive)* change entails conscious efforts by members to improve environmental standing or internal operations *before* pressure for change becomes acute. *Incremental changes* do not alter the main features of the seven system components, whereas *strategic changes* entail basic changes in one or more critical components and reworking of relations among components (Nadler & Tushman, 1989).

The Model as a Diagnostic Guide

The systems model reminds practitioners to consider all major system components when starting a diagnosis and not concentrate too soon on an evident and easy-to-study issue, such as morale or staff skills. The OS model thereby helps practitioners assess the broad context affecting operations within a particular organizational function, such as human resources. Similarly, the model can help practitioners assess the organizational context of specific problems or challenges, such as staff tensions stemming from the merger of two firms. By scanning the system characteristics of the client organization, practitioners can better understand both immediate and more distant forces affecting the focal problem or issue. Then, they can better define diagnostic problems that lie beneath presented problems. Moreover, they can concentrate most of their data gathering on those system components and subcomponents that are most directly related to the focal problem and most amenable to change.

By referring to the OS model, both managers and consultants may better resist the appeals of management fads that attribute organizational success mainly to one or two crucial features, such as quality, core business processes, leadership, or culture. The systems model also draws attention to interactions between system components and can guide the assessment of fit among components (see Chapter 4).

Many diagnostic models and techniques make system concepts more concrete and useful to managers. SWOT, which stands for strengths, weaknesses, opportunities, and threats, is a good example of these simple but powerful models (see Chapter 5). SWOT analysis is usually used to direct the attention of consultants and managers to crucial external challenges (threats and opportunities) and ways to enhance competitive advantage. The concepts in SWOT can also be defined more broadly to guide diagnosis of current success factors (i.e., strengths) and combinations of internal conditions (weaknesses) and external developments (threats) that may undermine success. Success factors are features that build an organization's capacity to obtain resources, process them efficiently while maintaining quality, and provide services or products that are valued by the environment. Success factors can also refer to features that contain unrealized potential for helping an organization make needed changes or enhance its environmental position. For example, a highly trained and flexible workforce could help a telecommunications firm develop new technologies or enter new markets. Weaknesses are internal forces that lead to ineffective performance or block efforts to enhance operations. Inflexible work rules and operating procedures would be a weakness for the firm just mentioned. Case 5 illustrates how the human resources function at CHF (see Case 2) was affected by these kinds of system strengths, weaknesses, and threats.

Case 5

Interviews suggested that the ability of CHF to provide health care rested substantially on the dedication of its nurses and medical aides, who persevered even though their work was not challenging, well paid, or prestigious. Many long-standing employees had strong ties to a local ethnic and religious community and had few alternative sources of local employment. These employees shared values that defined their work as fulfilling their moral obligation to care for people in need. Gradually, this organizational success factor was eroding as an external threat and internal weakness developed: Long-time employees were aging and were gradually being replaced by younger staff members. The new recruits were less tied to the local community, less committed to its religious values, and less dedicated to their work. In consequence, the human resource subsystem at CHF faced a growing problem: Turnover was increasing, and CHF was facing difficulties in recruiting nurses and medical aides. By restructuring CHF, its director hoped to solve some of these problems: He assumed that if CHF became more professionalized, it could more readily recruit and retain younger, better-trained nurses.

If developments within an organization or its environment are eroding the basis for past successes, as was occurring at CHF, consultants and clients must decide whether incremental adjustments in one or more system components will preserve or enhance effectiveness or whether more fundamental, strategic changes are needed. Then, clients and consultants can seek feasible routes to improvement, as CHF's director did.

When gathering and analyzing data for focused diagnoses such as the one previously described, practitioners initially examine the impacts of all system components on the focal problem. They may thus help clients break out of familiar ways of interpreting problems and discover more feasible solutions than those previously considered. Suppose, for example, that the customers and management of a resort hotel complain about the quality of guest service. The hotel manager attributes the problem to the hotel's inability to recruit experienced staff (a problem with human resource inputs), which stems from noncompetitive wage rates (a structural feature). By searching for links between the presented problem and other system components, the consultant might find weaknesses in employee training programs and definitions of job responsibilities (additional structural features), use of outmoded equipment (technology), and inadequate coordination and control of work (structures and processes). Improvements in these areas could enhance the quality of employee service, regardless of the employees' past work experience.

Redefining Presented Problems

The systems model can also help practitioners redefine problems or challenges initially presented by clients. Redefinition occurs whenever consultants treat problems presented as symptoms of broader or more fundamental conditions. The decision to examine all system components in a broad diagnosis includes an assumption that the forces behind presented problems or shaping organizational effectiveness may lie beyond the issues initially presented by the client. In the CHF study (Cases 2 and 5), the practitioner assumed that the proposed organizational transformation could only succeed if the entire system changed. Hence, he investigated system features that were not originally specified by the clients. Moreover, because leadership plays a crucial role in organizational transformation, the consultant closely examined this system subcomponent even though the clients had not expressed concern about it.

Although helpful, the OS model will not suggest precisely how to redefine a problem or how to go about solving it. Insights will typically derive more from past consulting experience and training, ideas generated by members of the organization, and the leads provided by some of the more explicit diagnostic models discussed in subsequent chapters and elsewhere (Burke & Litwin, 1992; Faletta & Combs, 2002; Harrison & Shirom, 1999; Howard & Associates, 1994).

GATHERING AND ANALYZING DATA

Basic Organizational Information

The list that follows, which draws on OS concepts and the work of Levinson (1972, 2002), provides basic information about a client organization (or subunit); this information is usually gathered during the entry phase of diagnosis and the early part of the data-gathering stage:

1. *Background to diagnosis:* initiator of contact with consultants; main clients; problems and challenges presented by contact person and other key figures; their explanation for problems; and recent major organizational successes and failures, as viewed by key figures

2. *Outputs:* mix and quantities of main products/services; rough quality indications, such as reputation and ratings; and indications of human outcomes, such as absenteeism, turnover, and safety

3. *Goals and strategies:* official statements of goals, strategies, and mission; recent and past changes in these areas; and actual priorities as indicated by budget allocations to divisions, programs, and functions (e.g., percentage of budget allocated to research and development)

4. *Inputs:* revenues and allocations from sales, services, and funding sources (e.g., for agencies); financial assets and capital assets, including real estate, physical plant, and equipment (amount and condition); and human resources—numbers of employees by job category, social and educational backgrounds, prominent occupational groups, training, and previous experience

5. *Environment:* affiliation and ownership (public vs. private and affiliation with larger bodies and nature of relations with them); outsourcing practices; alliances with other organizations (legal agreements and informal traditions of cooperation); main organizations and conditions in task environment; availability of funds for growth and expansion (internal and external borrowing, and grants and budget prospects for public agencies); and physical and social surroundings (e.g., city center or suburban location, transportation, access to services, and neighborhood safety)

6. *Technology and work processes:* main production processes (unit, batch, mass, and continuous process) and main interdependencies (pooled, sequential, and reciprocal—see p. 88); uses of information technologies and automation; procedures used to treat or process people in service organizations; and available data on operational failures, accidents, wastage, and down time

7. *Structure:* major divisions and units; number of levels of hierarchy; basis for grouping of units (e.g., by functions and markets) and coordination mechanisms; spans of control; spatial distribution of units, employees, and activities; unions and other forms of employee representation, labor contracts, grievance procedures, and human resource policies and practices; formal obligations affecting operations (e.g., affirmative action rules and quality assurance standards); and prominent power blocks and coalitions

8. *Behavior and processes:* main patterns of high-level decision making, strategy formulation, and planning; major types of conflicts, such as labor relations and conflicts between divisions; strength of unions and degree of militancy and employee involvement in issues other than compensation; and communication styles (e.g., oral, written, and meeting oriented)

9. *Culture:* symbols of organizational identity (logo, slogans, advertising campaigns, and physical appearance of corporate headquarters and branches); myths (e.g., stories of founders and historic successes); rituals (e.g., outings, celebrations, annual reviews, and plans); jargon (frequently used terms and phrases); dominant styles of dress, decor, and lifestyle; and prevailing practices (e.g., emphasis on teamwork) and work styles (e.g., long hours)

10. *System dynamics:* major changes in any system component during recent and more distant past; life cycle stage: entrepreneurial, collectivity, formalization, and structural elaboration (Quinn & Cameron, 1983); overall financial condition—profits, losses, and deficits; and growth and contraction in key system components (e.g., layoffs, sell-offs, and budget changes)

A few high-level managers or their assistants usually report on this basic information and provide access to available data and documentation. Statistics on topics such as budgets, workforce composition, financial position, and the scope of operations appear in organizational documents or can be prepared by staff members of the client organization after completion of the study contract. Whenever available, practitioners should also obtain official statements of the organization's mission and goals, charts of the organizational structure, and organizational histories. Site visits can provide some impressions of the organizational culture, such as the corporate image presented by buildings, equipment, and furnishings (e.g., state of the art or solid and traditional). Practitioners can also note the ways that employees dress, use jargon and terminology, and arrange their offices and work spaces (Steele, 1973). Subsequent investigations will be needed, however, to determine whether these artifacts and behavior patterns reflect everyday practices, unspoken assumptions, implicit values, or unwritten rules (Rousseau, 1990; Schein, 1997).

Additional Data

After gathering such preliminary information from the initial contact person and just a few other people, the practitioner usually plans interviews with top managers and heads of departments or divisions whose work is related to focal problems or challenges. Additional interviews, questionnaires, and focus groups may be used to understand the views and experiences of other members of units that affect central issues for diagnosis. This additional round of data gathering will provide richer and more valid information on basic system features and on underlying forces affecting presented problems and challenges. In most instances, these additional data will also reveal important differences in the ways that people from diverse functions, backgrounds, and levels view the organization and its problems.

A schedule such as the General Orientation Interview (Appendix A) can provide a starting point for these interviews. It covers characteristics of units and some broader organizational factors. Alternatively or as a supplement, investigators can construct schedules that focus on features of special interest. Standardized questions covering many of the topics listed under Basic Organizational Information and other important organizational features appear in the schedules described in Appendix B and are discussed in Chapter 3. Investigators can also follow the procedure explained in Chapter 5 to construct an interview guide for use in semistructured interviews.

Measurement

Because some of the factors covered in the Basic Organizational Information list and the General Orientation Interview are abstract and difficult to measure, practitioners must often content themselves with nonrigorous measures. For instance, when analyzing basic information about the organizational culture of a firm, a practitioner might make a judgment about the orientation toward employees conveyed in newsletters or other documents (e.g., hard-nosed and competitive or caring and supportive) without systematically coding the contents of the documents or interviewing managers and employees about human resource policies. More rigorous, but time-consuming, methods of gathering data should be contemplated only if the topic is particularly critical to the diagnosis. Likewise, practitioners often have to settle for global assessments of very complex conditions—including the organization's overall financial condition (ranging from excellent to critical), competitiveness of the environment, and degree of external threat or munificence.

To develop an independent assessment of organizational conditions, consultants will need to be aware of how respondents' descriptions are colored by their own distinctive views and experiences. One route to uncovering respondents' viewpoints and identifying controversial or problematic issues for further study is to compare how different respondents describe and interpret the same organizational and environmental conditions. To identify underlying interpretations and assumptions, practitioners can also ask respondents to provide brief narratives of the history of their organization (Leach, 1979). It is also helpful to solicit accounts of major organizational successes and failures so as to explore how respondents define success and failure and explain their causes (Argyris & Schon, 1995). Consultants can gain further insights about respondents' views by comparing their descriptions of ostensibly objective phenomena, such as the lines of authority and reporting. If, for example, departmental managers draw different organization charts of the same division, this diversity points to ambiguity and possibly to conflict about the lines of authority and the division of labor. By using two or more data-gathering methods on the same topic (e.g., analysis of corporate goals in the report to stockholders and in interviews) or multiple measures within a method, practitioners can also illuminate the perspectives and concerns of individuals and groups and thereby develop their own independent judgments about topics on which participants hold divergent views (Jick, 1979).

Summarizing and Analyzing Data

The lists of basic organizational information and system components can serve as accounting schemes for organizing and summarizing diagnostic findings. One straightforward approach is to make a separate file or database entry for each system component, noting the source of the information. A typical entry in the technology file for a diagnostic study of a high school might include a section, like the following, on instructional technologies:[1]

Instructional technology: Classes: most use lectures and discussions conducted by teacher, with blackboard illustrations and recording in notebooks; periodic use of traditional audiovisual equipment; rare use of simulations or Web-based sources for teaching (available only in Learning Center next to library). *Science laboratories* use microscopes, prepared slides, models, charts, Bunsen burners, ring stands, and chemicals. *Elective courses* on computer literacy, word processing, and programming use facilities of the Learning Center. *Learning Center:* 15 computers with limited capabilities (Windows 95; 16 mega memory—not suited for video editing or Web design), 7 newer computers (2002), and limited Internet access. *Remedial coaching* with computer-assisted instruction available in math and English. *Language laboratories:* two per week in French and Spanish—work stations with basic audio functions. *Library:* catalogue is digital; access to a few databases available only through librarian; insufficient technical support and maintenance. *Off-site:* stronger students ("about half") use e-mail, word processing, Internet, and Power Point extensively in homework exercises and projects. *Source:* assistant principal.

Except in very small organizations, divisions and other major subunits will probably differ substantially from one another in terms of system features, such as technology, structure, and processes. In addition, each major subunit usually deals with a different subenvironment within the organization's task environment. Hence, summaries should note the distinctive profiles of each division along with features common to the whole organization.

To summarize responses to interviews based on a schedule such as the General Orientation Interview, practitioners can start by grouping together responses to each question that make the same point and then record each type of response and the number of people giving it.[2] If, for example, 10 employees in a branch of a fast-food chain were interviewed, a typical entry in the summary might read like this:

Are there any difficulties or barriers to getting work done here or doing it the way you'd like to? (You can mention more than one.)

- Annoying customer complaints about food—taste, quality, etc. (3)
- Pressures from supervisor to work faster, come in on weekends (2)
- We often run out of buns or ketchup (4)
- Loud, disruptive customers (2)
- Sexual harassment by customers (3)
- No problems (3)

Popular word processing and database management programs, as well as programs designed for qualitative analysis (Lee & Fielding, 1998), can greatly facilitate the analysis of such descriptive data.

Practitioners can present the entire range of responses to specific questions as feedback to stimulate analysis of the operations and suggestions for improvement, or they can aggregate and summarize findings using accounting schemes such as SWOT or one based on the categories in the systems model. In the fast-food study, if the supervisor were to receive the feedback, the consultant would probably prefer not to summarize the response to separate questions. This kind of detailed summary might lead the supervisor to try to identify people who complained about their supervisor.

The systems model can also be used to direct attention to interactions between system components. A graphic approach that aids both analysis and feedback is to place all components in a circle and list their important subcomponents (e.g., processes such as rewarding, controlling, and conflict management). Color-coded lines can then be drawn between components or subcomponents that promote a focal condition, such as rapid employee turnover. Data supporting the inferences in the figure can be recorded separately and used appropriately in feedback. Investigators can diagnose environmental relations in terms of the effectiveness of current responses to the environment and the ability of the organization to deal with anticipated external developments. Chapters 3 through 5 provide more guidelines to diagnosing the organization as a system.

ASSESSING EFFECTIVENESS

Effectiveness is multidimensional (Denison & Mishara, 1995) and difficult to measure. For example, the effectiveness of health-care providers can be assessed in terms of very divergent criteria, each of which poses measurement challenges (Institute of Medicine, 2001). These include the cost of care, the degree to which it is appropriate (i.e., based on scientific knowledge and avoiding overuse and underuse), its safety, timeliness, equity, and patient centeredness. As is often the case in publicly contested areas, stakeholders—including government agencies, groups of providers, patient organizations, and consumer groups—assign divergent levels of importance to these criteria.

The OS frame, when supplemented by a view of organizations as political arenas and a systematic approach to concept development and measurement, can help consultants and decision makers make appropriate choices among the wide range of possible effectiveness measures.[3] In deciding how to define and measure effectiveness, practitioners of diagnosis face choices about five topics, listed here from the most general to the most specific:

1. Assessment approach
2. Domains (sets of conceptually related criteria)
3. Criteria
4. Operational definitions and measures
5. Standards for analysis and evaluation

Table 2.1 presents options for the first three sets of choices and provides a few illustrations (in parentheses) of operational definitions of specific criteria (Cameron, 1980; Kanter & Brinkerhoff, 1981; Lewin & Minton, 1986).

Assessment Approach

The first decision concerns the underlying assessment approach or combination of approaches. Each approach embodies very different images of an organization's ideal or preferred state and contains divergent assumptions about conditions promoting these states. Moreover, each approach leads to different assessment criteria.

Table 2.1
Effectiveness Criteria

Approach and Domains	Criteria
Output Goals	
Goal attainment	Achievement of main objectives (e.g., build Olympics site)
Outputs, quantity	Revenues, sales, numbers of services delivered, and profits
Outputs, quality	Reliability (rates of rejects, errors); service (e.g., tangibles, responsiveness, and courtesy); reputation (customer satisfaction, expert ratings); attainment of institutional standards (e.g., of quality assurance bodies)
Internal System State	
Efficiency and costs	Total costs, productivity (outputs per unit of cost or labor); efficiency measures (e.g., output value ÷ cost, with constant quality); wastage
Human outcomes	Quality of work life (Chapter 3); effort and commitment (turnover, absenteeism); employee health and safety; motivation, organizational image, and citizenship behavior
Consensus/conflict	Consensus on goals and procedures; cohesion and cooperation within and between units; conflict behavior (fights, protests, sanctions)
Flow of work and Information	Work coordination (flow of products, information between units; few delays, snags); adequacy, quality, and distribution of information
Interpersonal relations	Trust, reduction of status differences (perks, symbols); openness, honesty of communication; acceptance of diversity in background and orientations
Employee involvement	Participation in decision making; empowerment
Fits	Alignment of internal system components, subcomponents, and features
System Resources and Adaptation	
Resources, quantity	Size (employees, physical, capital, financial assets); resource flows (sales, budget allocations)
Resources, quality	Human capital (training, expertise); reputation of staff; knowledge base; desirability of clients (e.g., college selectivity)
Adaptation	Capacity to cope with external change and uncertainty; crisis management capability
Proactiveness	Impact on environment—clients, competitors, regulators, suppliers; entrepreneurialism; entry into new markets
Innovativeness	Technological and administrative innovation; implementation of new technologies and practices
Competitive position	Standing compared to competitors (market share, industry rankings); reputation for leadership in industry or sector
Fit	Alignment of internal system with environment

Approach and Domains	Criteria
Multiple Stakeholder Assessments	
Standards	Effectiveness domains and criteria, as selected and defined by stakeholders
Satisfaction	Satisfaction with organization on standards specified by stakeholders; stakeholders' overall level of satisfaction with organization

First, the output-goal approach derives from an instrumental frame, which views organizations as tools for goal attainment; this approach assesses effectiveness in terms of attainment of clearly defined objectives and production of specific outputs. In practice, organizations pursue multiple and even competing sets of goals and objectives, which are often advocated by divergent internal and external actors. Hence, several output-goal domains and multiple criteria specifying these domains can all be relevant to a single organization.

Second is a focus on Internal System States; it draws on the OS and human resources frames (Bolman & Deal, 2003). Sometimes, consultants and clients define internal system criteria, such as employee satisfaction and quality of work life, as ends in themselves. More often, consultants introduce these criteria into diagnosis because they assume that organizations can more readily attain their output goals when internal processes, such as coordination and communication, operate smoothly and efficiently and when these processes enhance the motivations and capacities of members.

The third approach stresses system resources and adaptation. It derives mainly from OS theories, which evaluate effectiveness in terms of the organization's ability to obtain scarce and valued resources from its environment, adapt to external change, and obtain a favorable competitive position within the environment.

The fourth approach focuses on assessments made by multiple stakeholders (constituencies). This approach defines effectiveness in terms of an organization's ability to satisfy a diverse set of internal and external constituencies (Connolly, Conlon, & Deutsch, 1980; Zammuto, 1984). Evidence indicates that organizations that are more responsive to the expectations of multiple stakeholders are generally more adaptable than comparable organizations in which less attention is given to stakeholders (Tsui, 1994). When the stakeholder approach is adopted, assessment of effectiveness begins with the identification of those groups or individuals who act as stakeholders for most of the actions of the organization or unit under study. The choice of stakeholding groups depends on the substantive focus of the diagnosis and on its level of analysis.

For example, a broad assessment of an electric company's organizational effectiveness might reasonably treat political groups fighting air and water pollution as company stakeholders. These same groups could be excluded from a narrower assessment of the company's human resource function.

Effectiveness Domains

The second decision concerns effectiveness domains. There are many possible sources of tension between domains that fall within the same theoretical frame and even among criteria drawn from a single domain. Moreover, in practice there may be little correlation between effectiveness domains or criteria from the same domain (Rousseau, 1997). Consider, for example, the domains listed under the System Resources and Adaptation heading in Table 2.1. Access to more revenues and budgetary flows may indeed be a sign that an organization effectively handles critical relations with external groups such as customers, banks, or governmental funding sources. Resource growth, however, can lead to ideological stagnation and the growth of hierarchies, processes that block adaptation to change and innovativeness. Similarly, there may be tensions between widespread employee involvement and administrative efficiency—two very different domains within the Internal System State grouping. No matter what type of effectiveness domains and criteria they use, people can simultaneously favor conflicting effectiveness standards. They may remain unaware of the conflicts between standards because they do not evoke them simultaneously or do not fully define their operational implications.

Criteria

The third decision concerns criteria for assessing each domain. The implications of any given assessment domain depend directly on the nominal definition of its criteria. An important case in point involves criteria for assessing service quality (Davenport, 1993, p. 266). Consider the quality of services provided by a unit that services copy machines: Quality includes tangibles, such as the appearance of personnel and service facilities; reliability of services rendered; responsiveness, including both timeliness and helpfulness; expertise of service personnel; and the courtesy with which personnel treat customers or clients. A service unit might be staffed with expert repair personnel and provide very reliable service while at the same suffer from lack of courtesy and slow responses to service calls.

If the multiple stakeholder approach is adopted, organizational effectiveness is defined as the ability to operate in ways that all stakeholders view as effective. The definition of what is meant by effective is left up to members of each stakeholder group. Employees in the copy service unit may agree with customers that service quality is a crucial aspect of unit effectiveness, but the employees might define quality in terms of expertise and reliability while overlooking courtesy, responsiveness, and tangibles.

Operational Definitions and Measurement

The fourth decision concerns the operational definition and measurement of effectiveness criteria. In principle, the procedure for deductively developing measures of effectiveness is identical to that of developing any kind of research measure. After clarifying the criterion at the nominal level, the investigator specifies what phenomena will be considered indicators of the criterion and chooses measures that derive logically from this operational definition.

Suppose that the practitioner who is assessing the photocopy service unit defines the criterion of service responsiveness in terms of timeliness. Timeliness is defined operationally and measured as elapsed time between service calls and service delivery. Then, a sample of clients could be asked to report how long they usually have to wait after placing a service call. The investigator might also calculate the time elapsed between receipt of calls and completion of service, as reported in the unit's service log. Although reasonable, these operational definitions neglect other aspects of responsiveness that may be very important to clients, such as the unit's responsiveness to calls for after-hours or weekend service or time spent on hold or punching in entries in a maze of voice mail options.

Diagnostic practitioners often have to define and measure effectiveness in ways that allow them to analyze available data or data that can be gathered quickly and inexpensively. Unless investigators keep clear conceptual and operational definitions of effectiveness in mind when working with these less than perfect data, they may interpret their findings incorrectly and overlook important phenomena that are not covered by these measures. An additional problem with available data arises when the measures were originally designed to evaluate the performance of employees or units. In such cases, members may have learned to perform in ways that make them look good on the measured criteria, such as the number of sales completed, while neglecting other desirable forms of behavior, such as customer satisfaction or service, that are less closely monitored.

The multiple stakeholder approach to assessing effectiveness rests on subjective assessments obtained from members of stakeholding groups. One assessment technique involves using an abstract measure, such as perceived organizational effectiveness, which allows respondents to refer to their own implicit definitions of effectiveness. An alternative technique involves asking representatives of major stakeholders to define effectiveness or select preferred definitions from a list of effectiveness criteria. This technique generates substantive data on the dimensions of effectiveness that are important to members of each stakeholding group, whereas the first technique only provides data on levels of stakeholder satisfaction.

Assessment of stakeholder views of ineffectiveness can follow a similar path. The diagnostic investigator directly asks members of important stakeholder groups to specify features of the organization's operations or its outcomes with which they are dissatisfied or that they view as ineffective. Then, for each ineffective feature, the investigator asks respondents a question such as, "What level of improvement [in the ineffective feature] would satisfy you?"

Standards for Analysis and Evaluation

The fifth choice relates to standards for analyzing and evaluating data on effectiveness and providing feedback (Cameron, 1980). Each of the following comparisons can generate standards for evaluation:

- Current versus past levels of effectiveness (e.g., rates of growth and development)
- Effectiveness levels among units within the same organization (e.g., comparisons of efficiency ratings, accidents, or quality)
- Client organization compared to others in the same industry or field (e.g., comparisons of profitability or sales to industry data)
- Current state versus some minimum standard (e.g., conformity to federal environmental standards)
- Current state compared to an ideal standard (e.g., innovativeness and community service)

Without standards, findings on effectiveness can be meaningless. For example, we can create an apparently objective measure of the productivity of a primary health-care clinic by calculating the number of patients treated per week divided by the number of full-time staff. However, we must have a standard, such as an average for strictly comparable units, to provide a basis for judging productivity.

The time frame used in assessments of effectiveness can vary from hours or days to years, depending in part on the organizational feature being assessed. Different time frames can also be applied to the same measure of effectiveness. For instance, a firm's financial performance may look good when judged in terms of its current quarterly profits or quarterly return on investment. However, if the firm achieves these results by aggressive cost cutting or pricing its services or products below market, it may be unable to sustain these results.

Moreover, neglect of investment in development of new products and services will gradually take its toll on sales and profits (Berenson, 2004; Hayes & Abernathy, 1980). Feedback containing appropriate comparisons can contribute directly to constructive problem solving. When data about an organization or unit are compared to data from other similar settings, the recipients of the data see that higher levels of effectiveness can be obtained and are motivated to try to improve their comparative standing. This type of comparison process underlies the techniques of survey feedback (Hausser, Pecorella, & Wissler, 1975) and also operates in many benchmarking activities. Comparisons of present levels of effectiveness or ineffectiveness to past ones can also generate motivation for change. Improvements over the past show that change is possible, whereas feedback on declining performance or growing ineffectiveness can sound an alarm that action is needed to halt further deterioration.

Making Choices About Effectiveness

Many considerations guide practitioners and their clients as they confront choices among effectiveness criteria (Cameron, 1984; Campbell, 1977; Connolly et al., 1980; Goodman & Pennings, 1980). These are summarized here under five guiding questions about effectiveness criteria.

First, how applicable and appropriate are particular effectiveness criteria to the focal organization? Output-goal measures are most applicable when goals can be defined in terms of clear, measurable objectives, and members of the client organization agree about the meaning and importance of these goals. Similarly, efficiency measures must be based on agreed-upon and accurate measures of inputs and quality of outputs, as well as on output quantity. In the absence of acceptable quality measures, it is risky to assume that improvements in productivity (outputs per input) signify the attainment of greater efficiency. Because they are so difficult to define and measure, output-goal criteria and efficiency measures are often not readily applicable to human services and cultural organizations.

Stakeholder criteria are particularly appropriate to organizations in which strategic decisions are highly contested, stakeholders are vocal and powerful. Moreover, there is increasing normative support for the view that internal and external stakeholders have legitimate interests in the contents and processes of corporate activities (Donaldson & Preston, 1995). These stakeholders include customers, employees, community members, and disadvantaged groups—not just stockholders and owners.

System adaptation and resource criteria are easier to apply in diagnoses in which clients are high-level managers, who have the authority to try to improve the environmental standing of an entire organization or semiautonomous division. In contrast, the criteria dealing with Internal System States can be applied to departments or subunits with little control over their environments. Criteria relating to smooth internal processes and cooperative relations are particularly relevant when work requires high levels of mutual consultation and adjustment, such as in professional and management teams. Concentrating exclusively on internal system criteria may lead consultants and clients to underestimate the importance of environmental challenges. Furthermore, focusing mainly on internal harmony and smooth coordination can distract attention from ways that internal pluralism, tension, and conflict can contribute to organizational adaptation. Internal conflict may be too low, rather than too high, when work standards are lax, members submit automatically to authority, or they avoid confronting the challenges and problems facing their organization (Robbins, 1978).

Second, how well do specific effectiveness criteria fit the goals and setting of the diagnostic study? The criteria vary in their applicability to particular types of organizations and the problems facing them. For example, system resource measures are likely to be appropriate to a diagnosis of a voluntary social service organization facing declining support from local government. Adaptation and innovation criteria are particularly appropriate to technology-intensive firms and to organizations facing difficulties keeping up with the changing expectations of customers or stakeholders. The internal system approach is likely to fit a diagnosis focused on ineffective coordination between departments.

Third, how relevant are effectiveness criteria to clients? Support for diagnosis and motivation to act on feedback increase when the study includes criteria that clients use in decision making and powerful stakeholders apply when they evaluate the organization's performance. Hence, diagnostic practitioners need to choose their basic assessment approach, effectiveness domains, and criteria so that they will best contribute to the strategic decisions facing clients (Campbell, 1977). To conduct a sharp-image diagnosis (see Chapter 1), consultants use effectiveness concepts to develop measures that generate feedback that directly addresses the goals of the diagnosis and helps clients understand the sources of the problems and challenges that concern them most. For instance, measures of output-goal attainment, efficiency, and inefficiency in work and information flows speak directly to the concerns of many business clients. To identify criteria favored by clients, consultants can directly ask them what measures they use in decision making and which matter most to them.

There is a fourth, related issue to consider in making choices about effectiveness: Are there strong normative or value reasons for preferring particular criteria, measures, or comparison standards? As the discussion of stakeholder assessment indicated, norms and values in and around an organization can lead investigators to favor one assessment technique or procedure over another. In other instances, norms may rule out use of particular measures or criteria. For example, hospital physicians may adamantly oppose giving out information about medical errors because the information might expose the physicians or their colleagues to malpractice claims.

Fifth, and perhaps most important, will feedback based on the selected criteria contribute to constructive problem solving? Diagnostic feedback aids organizational improvement and client learning when it leads recipients to decide which organizational features, if any, require improvement; what steps to take toward improvement; and how to assess progress toward change targets. Rather than galvanizing members toward action, feedback can foster confusion and discourage action if it is difficult to analyze, uses contradictory assessment criteria, or points to too many needed improvements. Assessments of stakeholder satisfaction often suffer from limitations such as these. Feedback on stakeholder divergence may leave clients wondering how to cope constructively with gaps in stakeholder priorities and ratings. When feedback data only give levels of stakeholder satisfaction, clients are left in the dark as to the basis for stakeholder ratings and ways to improve them.

To contribute to constructive problem solving, consultants may identify a limited number of assessment criteria on which clients and powerful stakeholders agree. When consensus about effectiveness remains illusive, consultants sometimes ask clients to develop a working agreement about organizational priorities. If this approach is impractical, consultants may use effectiveness criteria that are compatible with those of powerful stakeholders, even though they are not identical to them. Consultants further build support for their recommendations by suggesting organizational changes that will benefit the broadest possible spectrum of members and stakeholders and harm as few people as possible.[4]

Assessment and feedback about *in*effectiveness, as opposed to effectiveness, often produces more consensus among decision makers, leads more directly to action planning, and creates more motivation for change (Cameron, 1984; Taylor, 1991). For example, members of public-sector organizations often disagree on organizational goals and effectiveness criteria, but they agree on the need to cope with external threats, such as budget cuts or interference from pressure groups. Moreover, members of an organization facing a threat are more likely to agree on the actions needed to cope with threats. Even groups in direct conflict with one another may accept measures needed to save their firm from going broke or enduring a hostile takeover (Weitzel & Jonsson, 1989). In situations such as these, consultants foster motivation for action by providing clients and other stakeholders with data showing the organizational costs of ineffectiveness and the risks of continuing to perform poorly.

By concentrating on reducing ineffective outcomes, consultants can often tie their analysis more closely to the initial problems and challenges that clients presented. Solving problems stemming from ineffectiveness also contributes more directly and dramatically to organizational survival and short-term success.

Data on ineffectiveness are especially likely to promote constructive problem solving when they call attention to group and systemwide outcomes and processes, which can be improved through cooperation, rather than pointing to the inadequacies of individuals or small groups of people. The latter type of data feed into cycles of blame and defensiveness that can block problem solving and action.

ASSESSING FEASIBILITY OF CHANGE AND CHOOSING APPROPRIATE INTERVENTIONS

The political and open systems frames can help practitioners and their clients decide what steps, if any, will help clients solve problems and enhance organizational effectiveness.

Analytic and Process Issues

To make such an assessment, practitioners need to consider several questions.[5]

Does the Organization Need Incremental or Strategic Change?

Many organizational improvements emerge gradually through incremental steps (Weick & Quinn, 1999). Strategic changes, which are more episodic, include mergers, internal structural reorganizations, major financial cutbacks or new investment programs, fundamental changes in rules and processes (e.g., reengineering), and upgrading of major technologies. Top managers usually undertake strategic changes in response to major changes in environment (including ownership), technology, or performance that create pressure for fundamental change. Less frequently, strategic changes anticipate such developments. Strategic changes are difficult to accomplish and entail substantial risks because they usually require major investments or reallocations of budgets and can have widespread and unanticipated consequences.

Strategic changes are often needed when an organization undergoes decline (Cameron, Sutton, & Whetten, 1988) or is very likely to decline without suitable anticipatory action. Strategic change is also needed when incremental changes have become inadequate or are likely to become so in the near future.

Troubleshooting procedures and organizational routines are probably inadequate if an organization has fallen into a state of permanent crisis, lurching from one troubleshooting episode to another, or if short-term solutions to problems create long-lasting havoc in the organization. Moreover, organizations probably need strategic change if financial losses or customer satisfaction or other signs of ineffectiveness persist or become worse, despite repeated applications of quick and easy techniques.

By anticipating the need for strategic change, managers can more readily consider a range of possible actions and adjust their interventions on the basis of preliminary feedback concerning implementation. In contrast, if managers plan strategic changes only when declines or crises occur, they will have fewer options and encounter more severe constraints.

Is There Readiness for Change?

Members of an organization and external stakeholders often realize that something must be done to change an organization when they confront mounting signs of ineffectiveness or miss out on opportunities. Nonetheless, people and groups may legitimately worry that proposed changes will harm them. Diagnostic feedback may increase readiness for change by showing that problems are more severe than people had thought.

How Will Internal and External Stakeholders React to Proposed Interventions?

Proposals for interventions can come from consultants, clients, other members of the organization, controlling organizations, and external stakeholders. To assess the probable impacts of interventions, practitioners need to decide how the groups affected by the proposed steps are likely to react to them.[6] In particular, consultants should try to determine whether key decision makers and other powerful constituencies support or resist proposed interventions and are likely to provide the backing and resources needed to implement them.

What if diagnosis reveals that a particular form of intervention will probably encounter serious resistance by clients or by internal or external stakeholders? In this case, consultants can help clients explore ways to unfreeze resistance and build support for the proposed change (Chin & Benne, 1985). For instance, consultants and top managers can sometimes help rival power groups discover common interests, such as ensuring competitiveness in the global marketplace, and work together toward mutually beneficial solutions. When specific interventions create resistance, clients and consultants should seek alternatives that can serve equally well as levers for change but that are less threatening and better fit the needs and concerns of the affected groups.

Consultants might, for example, suggest that management retrain and reassign employees whose jobs will be eliminated by a planned merger of two divisions. Unfortunately, organizational change often threatens the basic interests of some groups. When this occurs, top management usually imposes change rather than implementing it through participatory decision processes (Dunphy & Stace, 1988). Consultants to clients who must impose change can help them examine the possible effects of alternative ways of handling resistance, such as bargaining, threats, and sanctions to force compliance (Kotter & Schlesinger, 1979).

Does the Organization Have the Capacity to Implement Change?

In diagnosing prospects for change, practitioners also need to assess whether the client organization has the capacity to implement proposed interventions. Capacity for change becomes particularly critical when organizations must undergo a lengthy transition before they can reach the desired future state (Beckhard & Harris, 1977; Bridges, 1991). To make a preliminary assessment of implementation capacity, practitioners can check whether each component of the system is likely to make the contributions required for successful implementation. To find out, consultants can consider questions such as these:

- Does the organization have the resources—people, funds, skills, knowledge, and technology—needed to implement proposed interventions? Can it obtain or develop the resources it lacks?
- Can adjustments in current organizational and technical arrangements accommodate and facilitate implementation (e.g., through the creation of teams or project groups to manage the change)?
- Will dominant behavior patterns, processes, beliefs, and values in the organizational culture fit those required by the change program?
- Will the environment provide the necessary support, permission, and resources?

Will the Proposed Interventions Achieve the Desired Results Without Having Undesirable Consequences?

Before recommending interventions, practitioners should make a final accounting of the probable benefits and risks of each possible move. By considering likely impacts of proposed interventions on system components and on interactions among them, consultants estimate whether interventions are likely to produce desired consequences without creating others that are both unintended and undesirable. Planned changes are more likely to succeed if they fit key conditions in the client organization or the organization can "stretch" its capacities and procedures to meet new challenges (Hamel & Prahalad, 1994). Consider, for example, a proposed merger between two firms that have very different corporate cultures. Gaps between accepted practices and operating assumptions in the staffs of the two firms can undermine relations between them (Buono & Bowditch, 1989) unless ways can be found to bridge the culture gap and ensure good working relations.

Consultants should weigh carefully the likely positive and negative effects of any interventions that might produce lasting improvements in effectiveness. If time permits, they can recommend incremental interventions that require low levels of initial support and commitment and are less likely than major changes to encounter serious resistance or lead to other undesirable consequences (Schaffer, 1988). If these small steps succeed, more ambitious changes can be considered subsequently. When time is short or small steps will not suffice, consultants and clients must search for the interventions most likely to produce vital improvements and chart ways to handle any anticipated resistance.

Methodological Issues

Because it is difficult to predict behavior only from general attitudes (Ajzen, 2001; Sutton, 1998), people's broad reactions to a proposed intervention do not provide sufficient guidance as to how they will act after the intervention is implemented. Social pressures from peers or supervisors can make people hesitate to reveal their true feelings. Moreover, people's initial attitudes toward a change may shift during its implementation, as they discover that the costs and benefits of the change differ greatly from what they had anticipated. Despite these drawbacks, attitudinal data can reveal previously unnoticed hostility toward programs of change. In addition, interviews with powerful individuals who represent key constituencies may indicate whether they will support or resist an intervention. Influential leaders who lack formal authority should also be included in such interviews.

To move beyond attitudinal assessments, consultants can also examine the ways that members reacted in the past when changes were introduced. If practitioners and clients carefully consider the nature of past interventions and the procedures used to introduce these interventions, they may be able to learn what types of interventions are most feasible and which procedures are best for implementing them.

Because it is difficult to anticipate the consequences of interventions and people's reactions to them, managers and consultants sometimes adopt a more experimental approach to implementation. They may, for instance, implement a program in stages, beginning with some preliminary activity (such as off-site meetings with top managers to plan changes) to better understand members' reactions, deal with them at each stage, and anticipate future reactions. By obtaining frequent feedback on implementation, managers can make program adjustments or even reassess their entire plan of action. Alternatively, management may introduce administrative or technological changes as experiments in one or more units within an organization. During this trial period, the people responsible for implementing change often modify the original interventions. After a trial period and an assessment of the consequences, the innovation is further modified and then diffused to other parts of the organization. Unfortunately, managers in both the public and the private sector sometimes agree to introduce such a pilot program to show that they are forward looking, although they have little real intention of extending the program to the rest of the organization. An additional drawback to experimental programs is that the enthusiasm created by the newness and uniqueness of the program can wear off when the change is introduced widely and becomes well established.

EXERCISES

1. Basic Organizational Information

Locate a person who is very knowledgeable about an organization and willing to serve as a contact person. Interview this person to obtain as much basic organizational information as possible. Find out from the contact person what other sources could provide additional basic organizational information. Pay close attention to documentary and statistical information. Prepare a plan for corroborating the information received and collecting additional information.

2. General Orientation Interviews

Plan a general orientation interview (Appendix A) that concentrates on the unit (e.g., department) in which the person being interviewed works. Note in advance which questions are inappropriate and will be skipped and which will need rewording to make them more applicable. Do not spend more than 1 hour on this first interview. Write a report in which you summarize technical and procedural difficulties encountered in conducting the interview (e.g., keeping the respondent on track, time pressures, and skipped questions). Explain how you would deal with these difficulties during the next interview. After getting feedback on your report from your instructor, conduct two more interviews with members of the same unit or similar ones, and summarize the findings in terms of the headings provided in Appendix A (e.g., The Person and His or Her Job).

3. Effectiveness Criteria

Conduct an open, semistructured interview with one of the people in charge of an organization (or unit). Ask the person to describe an example of successful operations in the organization. Then ask what the general objectives are toward which members strive and how they know whether they are achieving them. Based on these responses and any other data (e.g., impressions from previous exercises),

- specify the effectiveness criteria to which the respondent referred;
- explain whether these criteria reflect considerations of output, system state, adaptation, or stakeholder satisfaction;
- suggest additional effectiveness and ineffectiveness criteria that would fit the expressed priorities and needs of those in charge of the organization;
- note criteria that reflect the interests of other internal and external stakeholders and criteria, such as ineffectiveness, on which consensus might be achieved. Explain your choices.

NOTES

1. This illustration draws in part on Selingo (2003).

2. For content analysis techniques, see Neuendorf (2002) and Weber (1990).

3. For more detail on the development of effectiveness concepts and their measurement, see Harrison and Shirom (1999).

4. In deciding how to deal with clients who favor or use conflicting standards of effectiveness, diagnostic practitioners should bear in mind that many organizations develop structures that separate units or functions having conflicting management systems and priorities (Chapter 4, this volume; Orton & Weick, 1990). Moreover, some research indicates that organizations are most effective when they simultaneously balance competing values and satisfy multiple performance criteria (Cameron & Quinn, 1988; Denison & Spreitzer, 1991; Quinn & Rohrbaugh, 1983).

5. Based in part on Burke (1982, pp. 215–233) and President and Fellows of Harvard College (1980).

6. See Exercise 4 in Chapter 4, this volume, and Harrison and Shirom (1999, pp. 117–132) on applications of stakeholder analysis (Savage, Nix, Whitehead, & Blair, 1991) and force field analysis.

3

Assessing Individual and Group Behavior

In this chapter, a system model is provided to guide the assessment of individual and group behaviors and their impact on organizational effectiveness. Individual, group, and organizational forces shaping behavior are considered. Human resource management programs, which are designed to shape organizational behavior, are among the organizational forces examined. Then, a model is presented that focuses on conditions influencing critical group processes and performance outcomes. Techniques for gathering, analyzing, and feeding back data are also discussed. Special attention is given to the use of standardized questionnaires.

Why do some service teams earn praise from clients, while others get nothing but complaints?

We are losing top staff people, but the less promising ones stay on.

Our weekly program review meetings have deteriorated to the point where we argue repeatedly about the same issues and never get anywhere.

We need to know whether our staff development programs are producing managers who can lead our firm's expansion into the global marketplace.

The first three of these statements illustrate typical problems and challenges that clients present to behavioral science consultants. All three concern the possible effects of individual or group (team) behavior on organizational effectiveness.[1] The fourth statement asks for an assessment of whether a human resource management program is building staff skills.

MODEL FOR DIAGNOSING INDIVIDUAL AND GROUP BEHAVIOR

Many forces in and around organizations shape patterns of organizational behavior such as those illustrated in the previous statements. Figure 3.1

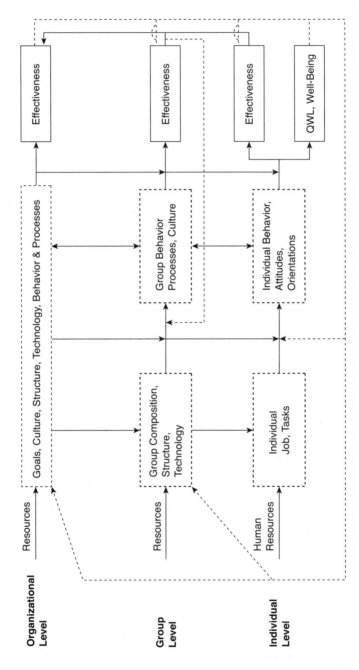

ENVIRONMENT

Organizational Level

Group Level

Individual Level

Resources

Goals, Culture, Structure, Technology, Behavior & Processes

Effectiveness

Resources

Group Composition, Structure, Technology

Group Behavior Processes, Culture

Effectiveness

Human Resources

Individual Job, Tasks

Individual Behavior, Attitudes, Orientations

Effectiveness

QWL, Well-Being

Figure 3.1   Model for Diagnosing Individual and Group Behavior

Key: Solid lines show main lines of influence. Broken lines show feedback loops.

summarizes a guiding system model of the important forces and outcomes to examine in diagnosis.[2] A broad diagnosis would encompass the whole range of factors shown in the figure. A focused diagnosis would consider the subsets that were found to be important during entry and that closely reflected client concerns. The arrow in Figure 3.1 for human resource inputs refers to characteristics and traits that employees acquired in the past. The two boxes in the center of the bottom row depict the main forms of organizational behavior that shape group and individual outcomes. The outcomes shown in the figure include organizational, group, and individual effectiveness, along with quality of work life (QWL) and well-being. QWL refers to the degree to which work contributes to employees' material and psychological well-being (Nadler & Lawler, 1983; Walton, 1975). For simplicity, the model does not distinguish between divisional and organization-level phenomena, but this distinction may be important if divisions differ substantially from one another.

Effectiveness

The critical aspects of individual and group effectiveness for diagnosis depend on the primary problems and challenges facing the groups and their main tasks, goals, and standards. Despite their limitations, output criteria are understandably popular. To assess group effectiveness in terms of outputs, consultants need to define the most important goods or services produced by the group and measure their output quality and quantity over a given time period. For instance, to assess quantitative outputs among units within state employment security offices, one researcher (Gresov, 1989, p. 441) counted claims processed by intake and processing units, job seekers placed by placement units, and people counseled by employment counseling units. The outputs for administrative and professional teams with complex tasks are often difficult to measure. They include solutions to problems (e.g., how to increase market share), plans (e.g., plans for AIDS education in the schools), tactics, and procedures for coordinating the work of other units.

Individual effectiveness includes the degree and quality of members' efforts, their level of initiative, cooperation with other employees, absenteeism, lateness, and commitment to the job. QWL and well-being are often defined in terms of employees' levels of satisfaction with the following conditions:

- Job security
- Fairness and adequacy of pay
- Working conditions
- Interpersonal relations
- Meaningfulness and challenge of work

Investigators can obtain descriptions of working conditions from employees or rate QWL and other working conditions on the basis of observation or the judgments of experts. Diagnosis can also use objective and subjective indicators of individual health and well-being, including rates of job-related illness, accidents, substance abuse on or off the job, stress, and burnout (Cook, Hepworth, & Wair, 1981, pp. 98–112; Cooper, 1998; Danna & Griffin, 1999; Maslach, Schaufeli, & Leiter, 2001; Shirom, 2003). Satisfaction with rewards may be valued for its own sake or because job satisfaction often reduces both desire for withdrawal from the job and turnover (Fisher & Locke, 1992). Under certain conditions, improvements in QWL and employee well-being can also lead to cost savings and higher productivity (Katz, Kochan, & Weber, 1985; Walton, 1975).

Factors Affecting Individual and Group Effectiveness

Many individual-level factors affect individual and group effectiveness (see Figure 3.1). These include member characteristics such as education and training, the design of jobs, employee motivations, and attitudes to specific organizational actions and issues (e.g., mergers and diversity training). The impact of such individual factors can best be investigated directly because many factors intervene to shape how they influence group and individual outcomes. Such factors are most critical for organizational diagnosis when they are shared by sizable groups of employees. For example, the increase in educational levels among blue-collar workers throughout Europe and North America led workers to prefer more interesting and challenging work.

Despite the influence of such human resource inputs, practitioners and clients should not overestimate their importance. It is sometimes tempting to assume that the problems of a failing program or department could be solved if only the "right person" could be found to run it or the right staff members were chosen. When a unit's problems seem likely to persist even if the "ideal" manager and staff are found, group and organizational sources of the problem also require investigation. Practitioners should also consider group and organizational factors when clients cannot readily alter individual factors and human resource inputs (e.g., when employees have civil service tenure).

By examining employees' expectations and understandings of their work situation, consultants may discover explanations for suboptimal performance. If people expect their efforts to go unrewarded or to yield rewards that are not important to them (e.g., citation in the company newsletter), they will remain unmotivated to work toward improvement.

Diagnoses can also benefit from the assessment of specific attitudes and perceptions about questions being debated within an organization, such as a merger or a new outsourcing policy. Consultants might, for example, ask employees how they feel about an outsourcing policy so as to assess the policy's impact on staff morale and turnover intentions. Repeated attitude surveys can also provide feedback on particular programs or groups. This information can contribute to assessment of progress toward a stated goal and can help managers spot problems before they become critical.

Group composition, structure, and technology can decisively shape individual, group, and organizational outcomes. For example, teams that are more heterogeneous on factors such as social background, education, and occupation are often more creative than more homogeneous groups but can also be less cohesive and less satisfying to participants (Milliken & Martins, 1996). Diagnostic studies often trace ineffective behavior to structural and technological factors at the group and organizational levels. For example, a diagnosis might reveal that the reward system encourages one type of behavior, such as individual productivity, while top management continues to hope for some other kind of outcome, such as enhanced teamwork (Kerr, 1995). Diagnoses can also uncover failures to measure critical outcomes. For instance, if long-haul freight crews are evaluated on down time and damage levels of delivered freight, they may learn to improve their ratings by cutting down on time-consuming safety checks. Other potentially influential group factors to consider include communication processes, cooperation and conflict, decision making, supervisory behavior, and group norms and beliefs. Research has shown much variation in the impacts of factors such as these on individual and group performance (Guzzo & Dickson, 1996).

Diagnostic studies can profitably explore the effects on individual and group effectiveness of a broad range of organizational factors. These include strategies, standards, and goals, which help shape the targets that managers use to evaluate performance. Attention is also warranted to the ways that organizational technologies and structures shape coordination and control within groups, the division of labor within and between groups, and the content of team and individual tasks.

Organizational culture is another factor that can affect performance. Culture shapes the beliefs and assumptions that focus people's attention and channel their effort (Ashkenasy, Wilderom, & Peterson, 2000; Trice & Beyer, 1993). Chief among these are beliefs about the way work gets done, how change occurs, who is powerful, what clients and customers expect, and how external trends and developments affect the organization. For example, in high-reliability organizations (Weick & Sutcliffe, 2001), members avoid potentially disastrous accidents and mistakes through intense awareness of possible causes of mistakes and consistent efforts to eliminate error-prone behavior.

Human Resource Management Programs

In addition to the broad organizational factors previously discussed, diagnosis can examine human resource management (HRM) activities. These are programs and actions that are intended to shape the skills, knowledge, attitudes, and behavior of employees. A broad assessment of HRM impacts would encompass major HRM activities, including the following:

- External staffing (recruitment and selection)
- Internal staffing (placement, promotion, discharge, and retirement)
- Compensation (pay and benefits)
- Labor relations (contract negotiation and administration, grievances, and employee rights)
- Work environment (job design and occupational health and safety)

The following supporting HRM operations may also be investigated:

- Goal setting
- Planning (linking HRM to organizational strategy and goals; forecasting trends and planning actions)
- Job analysis (skill requirements, rewards, and motivational potential)
- Evaluation and performance assessment

More problem-oriented and focused diagnoses could treat one or more of these HRM areas as the main object for investigation (Harrison & Shirom, 1999, pp. 209-234). Case 6, for instance, presents an illustration of how a consultant might diagnose management training and development programs within a firm moving toward transnational operations—a complex, decentralized set of operations in many countries with many strategic alliances to local firms.[3]

Case 6

To start, the practitioner defines the skills needed for managing a truly transnational firm. Among these skills is the ability to interact simultaneously with people from many cultures, learn from them, and treat them as equals. The practitioner then examines whether training programs, on-the-job experiences, and career development among the firm's managers are likely to foster these skills. To assess the impacts of training programs, the practitioner checks whether curriculum and instructional techniques are designed to promote the needed skills. If so, the practitioner directly measures training outcomes to see whether these formal objectives are achieved in practice. Recommendations focus on closing the gap between current and desired practices to enhance skill development. Management might, for example, increase multinational participation in training programs and treat international experience and cultural adaptability as important criteria for career development and promotion.

ACTION MODEL FOR GROUP TASK PERFORMANCE

To simplify diagnosis and intervention, Hackman and colleagues (Hackman, 1987, 1991) developed the Action Model for Group Task Performance. Instead of encompassing the entire range of factors in Figure 3.1, the model focuses on organizational and group conditions that can serve as change levers for improving the task performance of work groups.[4] These conditions can serve well both as focal points for diagnosis and as building blocks in the design of new work groups.

At the center of the model, which is depicted in Figure 3.2, lie the following three critical group processes that pose the major hurdles to effective group performance:

1. Exertion of enough joint effort to accomplish tasks at acceptable levels of performance

2. Bringing adequate skills and knowledge to bear on the work

3. Using task performance strategies that fit the work and the cultural and organizational setting in which the work is done

Assessment of how well groups handle these critical processes can provide valuable diagnostic information about the groups' capacity for meeting effectiveness targets. However, interventions that target conditions that facilitate critical group processes are more likely to enhance group performance than efforts to directly change group processes.

As Figure 3.2 shows, there are four sets of potentially facilitating conditions. Each identifies likely causes of ineffective group processes and outcomes and provides potential levers for intervention to improve group functioning and task performance (see also Hackman, 2002). First are conditions relating to the *organizational context* within which the group operates. Higher management can promote performance by defining goals for group performance that are challenging and specific. Performance is enhanced when management delegates to the team much authority for deciding how to attain these goals. Organizational *reward systems* promote performance by focusing on group actions and outcomes, rather than individual performance, and recognizing and reinforcing good performance. The organization's *information system* can provide access to data and forecasts that help members

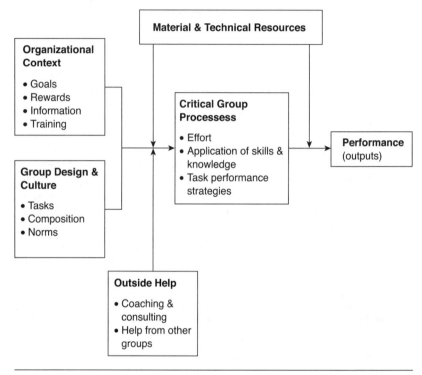

Figure 3.2   Action Model for Group Task Performance

formulate their tasks and their performance strategies and provide feedback on performance. Informal and formal *training systems* contribute to performance by providing members with the necessary skills and knowledge in advance of task activity and in response to members' needs.

Second, *group design and culture* can facilitate or hinder group processes and performance. The most critical *task conditions* for groups include defining clear tasks, setting challenging objectives, assigning shared responsibility, and specifying accountability for task performance. In addition, it is important that groups be as small as possible because larger groups encounter more coordination problems. *Compositional features* that contribute to performance focus include clear boundaries; inclusion of members who possess the needed skills and knowledge, including interpersonal skills; and creation of a good mix of members in terms of training and experience. This mix ensures cross-fertilization and creativity while avoiding insurmountable divergences of opinion and working styles. Finally, groups are more successful when they possess clear and strong *norms* that regulate behavior and ensure coordinated action. It is also important that these norms encourage members to act proactively and learn from their experiences.

Investigators can develop diagnostic questions based on each of the previously discussed facilitants of group processes. For example, diagnosis can assess whether managers set clear, challenging tasks for group members or fall into the trap of telling them to do their best, without specifying challenging, operational objectives. Diagnosis can also examine group and individual accountability for tasks so as to be sure that critical tasks are not falling between the cracks (see the discussion of responsibility charting in Chapter 4, pp. 79–81).

The third set of facilitating conditions refers to access to *outside help,* such as *coaching and consulting* received by members. Like team leaders, external coaches and consultants can help members anticipate or resolve critical coordination problems and learn to collaborate effectively. Coaches can also help build commitment to the group and its task. Leaders and coaches facilitate performance when they help members decide how best to use participants' skills and knowledge, learn from one another, and learn from other groups. Leaders or coaches also help groups avoid performance strategies that are likely to fail and can help group members think creatively about new ways to handle their tasks.

Fourth, groups need access to appropriate *material and technical resources.* Without the needed equipment, funds, or raw material, group outputs will be inferior, even if the group members perform well on all the process criteria. Furthermore, serious resource constraints and acute shortages can lead to frustration, and even turnover, among potential high performers and can erode a group's long-term performance capacity. Resource availability is particularly critical in groups that are undergoing structural change or learning new techniques for handling their tasks. Managers responsible for introducing change sometimes expect performance to improve immediately without investing in the necessary processes of learning, training, and experimentation that occur during change. By singling out material and technical resources as critical variables that intervene between group processes and performance, the Action Model reminds managers and consultants to pay attention to seemingly mundane issues in addition to examining the availability of needed human resources, knowledge, and information.

Drawing on the Action Model, diagnostic studies can examine whether current conditions in each of these four areas lead to ineffective or effective performance.[5] For example, basing their work substantially on Hackman's model, Denison, Hart, and Kahn (1996) developed and validated a set of diagnostic questionnaire items for members of cross-functional teams. These items ask respondents to report the degree to which their team enjoys supportive facilitating conditions, handles team processes effectively, and obtains desired outcomes. It is also possible to use the model to examine whether interventions by clients or consultants could appropriately concentrate on changing specific facilitating conditions or group processes.

Another way to use the model in diagnosis is to follow the problem-oriented, sharp-image logic explained in Chapter 1. The diagnosis would start with performance problems and then trace these signs of ineffectiveness back to difficulties in handling one or more critical group processes. Then, these difficulties can be followed back to the other elements in the model, such as group design and organizational context, which can hinder or facilitate group processes. For instance, a consultant or manager might trace problems of low quality in an industrial work group back to a critical process, such as pursuit of an inappropriate quality-assurance strategy. If the quality-assurance strategy is inappropriate, then the solution lies in redesigning the group's task (a facilitating condition) so as to include appropriate quality-assurance techniques. Suppose that the group did choose an appropriate strategy for quality assurance, but team members lack the skills and knowledge needed to implement the strategy. In this case, the solution lies in changing other conditions, such as coaching for skill use and development, training programs, or procedures for selecting team members.

Although the Action Model provides useful starting points for diagnosis, it does not reflect distinctive challenges and conditions facing divergent types of groups. The distinctive challenge for air traffic controllers, for example, is reliability, whereas a repertoire theater group faces problems of maintaining spontaneity and artistic vigor night after night. Similarly, groups and entire organizations face divergent challenges at different periods in their life cycles (Harrison & Shirom, 1999, pp. 299–324). Nor does the Action Model pay much attention to important "soft" aspects of group interaction, such as mutual expectations and understandings. An additional limitation is the model's heavy stress on measurable outputs, which could lead analysts and clients to pay less attention than needed to other dimensions of effectiveness and ineffectiveness. Finally, the Action Model builds in strong assumptions about the likely indicators and causes of ineffectiveness and the best ways to intervene to enhance group performance. Hence, the model may discourage users from attending directly to client concerns and from identifying causes and possible solutions that reflect the organization's distinctive features and the contingencies affecting it.

DIAGNOSTIC METHODS AND PROCEDURES

This section examines the design and administration of a diagnosis of forces affecting individual and group outcomes. It also notes general issues that arise in most diagnoses, no matter what questions or organizational levels are emphasized.

Study Design

Deciding What to Study

Consultants usually select topics for study in response to their clients' initial presentations of problems and in keeping with the preliminary diagnosis made during the entry period. For instance, the complaint about the argument-ridden, unproductive meetings cited at the beginning of the chapter might lead a consultant to explore the background to the arguments that plague the meetings. Preliminary conversations with participants might reveal major disagreements about program goals, along with a lack of mechanisms for working out such difficulties. In keeping with these findings, the consultant could explore goal-setting and decision-making processes more closely.

The choice of diagnostic topics also reflects the effectiveness criteria to be used in assessing individual and group behavior. In addition to the individual and group outcomes discussed in this chapter, many of the Internal System State criteria listed in Table 2.1 can serve as standards for evaluating work groups. Rancorous conflict, for example, can be treated as a sign of team ineffectiveness. Group effectiveness can also be evaluated in terms of capacity for satisfying the conflicting demands of multiple stakeholders (Tsui, 1990). Practitioners can apply some of the system resources and adaptation criteria (e.g., innovativeness and resource quality) in Table 2.1 to small groups by defining the group's environment as including other units within the focal organization along with parts of the organization's environment.

Having chosen a particular focus for diagnosis, the practitioner must define carefully the specific factors to be studied and decide on the best ways to obtain data on them. To start, practitioners can gather basic organizational information (see Chapter 2) and conduct a limited number of general orientation interviews (see Appendix A). They can design additional data-gathering steps as needed. For example, a consultant seeking to examine conflict management and problem solving could interview group members, paying particular attention to the kinds of issues that create conflicts and the ways that members and supervisors deal with these conflicts. These data might then be supplemented with observations of group meetings (see Appendix C).

Studies that focus on assessing HRM programs can compare data on actual practices to criteria derived from a goal statement or ideal standard (e.g., Case 6). Sometimes, a quasi-experimental design (Cook, Campbell, & Peracchio, 1991) may be used in HRM assessment. Suppose that the human resources unit of a large trucking firm sought to assess the effectiveness of a safety program that gives cash bonuses to safe drivers. If the investigators can arrange to have drivers randomly assigned to the new program, they can compare the accident and traffic violation records of program participants before and after participation in the program. These results will be compared to those of the nonparticipants during the same period. Follow-up will be necessary to determine whether program effects erode over time, as they often do.

Sampling

The data should be as representative as possible of the individuals, groups, and situations under study. For example, to discover the characteristic ways in which conflicts are handled, the practitioner would examine typical or representative conflict episodes and select a representative cross section of group members for interviews. To reach large numbers of people, self-administered questionnaires can be distributed to samples of members selected through probability sampling (Trochim, 2001). Probability samples can also be used to gather secondary data, such as absenteeism rates from large data sets. Practitioners rarely use complex probability sampling techniques to choose subjects for interviewing because of the high cost of conducting a large number of interviews. When small groups are to be interviewed or given questionnaires, all members are included, or a cross section of individuals are chosen who are likely to hold different perspectives.

In designing samples, practitioners of diagnosis consider the attitudes of group members toward the study and the uses to which the data will be put as well as strictly methodological considerations. If, for example, all members of a large division will receive feedback from a questionnaire about their departments' operations, it may be better to include everyone in the survey. By doing so, consultants may increase interest in the questionnaire study and enhance the believability of the feedback.

Data gathering through observation also raises sampling issues. Because large-scale observation is expensive and time-consuming, consultants usually prefer to observe important meetings, training sessions, or crucial work activities in which members interact intensively and many aspects of group relations can be seen at the same time (see Appendix C). It is best to choose settings for observation that are as central to group operations as possible because behavior can vary greatly from one context to another (e.g., headquarters vs. field operations). A unit may also operate differently when it convenes as a whole than it does when its members work alone or in subgroups.

Administering the Study

Procedures used to gather, store, and analyze the data should promote sound relations between consultants and members of the organization as well as provide valid diagnostic data. Practitioners should make it clear to members of a client organization that they will store and process the data professionally and maintain the confidentiality of participants. Moreover, they should explain that only group-level results will be reported to preserve the anonymity of individual members.

Measurement and Data-Gathering Techniques

By using a combination of data-gathering techniques, consultants can enhance the validity of their findings. The following discussion emphasizes questionnaires because of their popularity and appropriateness to the individual and group levels of analysis.

Analyzing Available Data

Practitioners can extract data on the social or personal characteristics of work group members from the personnel files of a client organization or ask to have such data prepared for them. Most for-profit organizations and an increasing proportion of not-for-profits also have records of group outputs, such as sales, productivity, product quality (e.g., percentage of products serviced under warranty), and services delivered (e.g., the number and type of outpatient visits to a hospital clinic). Organizational publications and records may also provide information on processes, structures, technologies, and purposes, but such information will be difficult to code and quantify. Documentary data almost always need to be supplemented with information on emergent practices (see Chapter 4).

Organizational documents or records frequently reflect the perspectives of those who gathered the information and the reasons for which it was originally gathered. Employee evaluations used to make decisions about pay raises, for example, may reflect pressures on immediate supervisors to present their subordinates in a favorable light. In contrast, negative comments about these employees by more senior managers may reflect a desire to avoid granting raises automatically. By examining both sets of views, the practitioner can better understand the ways that members of the focal organization interpret employee behavior and the factors shaping their interpretations. The practitioner cannot accept either set of evaluations as unbiased, however.

Interviews

Besides examining individual attitudes and behavior, interviews can include relevant questions on other topics from the General Orientation Interview (Appendix A), focus on selected human resource programs, or delve into critical group processes and outcomes. In seeking information about groups, divisions, or entire organizations, investigators need to pose questions that fit the positions and organizational level of respondents. For example, department heads may provide basic information on department regulations, history, and working relations with other departments; their subordinates may have little knowledge in such areas. In contrast, subordinates sometimes know better than their boss how work is actually done.

Interviews and questionnaire studies are often subject to bias because respondents seek to present themselves in a favorable light or withhold information that might be used against them, such as negative descriptions of supervisors. By conducting interviews with members from different backgrounds and locations within a unit and listening carefully to their accounts of important issues, investigators can become aware of members' distinct perspectives and viewpoints. For example, department heads might characterize their organization as dealing honestly and directly with employee grievances, whereas subordinates complain that their grievances are ignored or minimized by management. The people interviewed may be unaware of such a diversity of viewpoints or intolerant of the feelings and perceptions of others. In such cases, consultants can summarize the various viewpoints during feedback to stimulate communication and encourage people to respect diverse perspectives and opinions. In other instances, consultants can simply take note of divergent viewpoints and avoid giving undue weight to one particular interpretation when formulating their own descriptions and analyses.

By building relations of trust with group members, consultants can sometimes overcome people's reluctance to reveal sensitive information during interviews. Practitioners may also gain the trust of one or more members of an organization who are knowledgeable about organizational affairs but are somewhat detached from them.[6] Assistants to high-level managers, for example, often have a broad view of their organization and may be more comfortable describing it than are the top managers. When such well-placed individuals trust consultants, they may provide useful information about sensitive subjects, such as the degree of influence of managers who officially have the same level of authority or staff members' past reactions to risk-taking behavior. Gathering such sensitive information poses tricky ethical issues, several of which are discussed in Chapter 6.

Self-Administered Questionnaires

Self-administered questionnaires provide the least expensive way of eliciting attitudes, perceptions, beliefs, and reports of behavior from many people. Questionnaires can be administered in person or by mail, telephone, or Internet (Miller & Salkind, 2002; Stanton & Rogelberg, 2001). Aggregations of individual responses can also provide a substitute for behavioral measures of group and organizational phenomena. Although questionnaires typically use fixed-choice answers, a few open-ended questions can be included to give respondents an opportunity to express themselves. Responses to such open-ended questions are often informative but difficult to code. Questionnaires composed of items drawn from previous research studies and standardized organizational surveys can be prepared and administered rapidly because there is less need to develop and pretest the instrument. By including standard measures, consultants may also be able to compare the responses obtained in the client organization with results from other organizations in which the same instrument was used.

Standardized Instruments

Many standardized organizational survey instruments have been developed, which can be used in diagnostic studies (see Appendix B). Examples include the well-documented Michigan Organizational Assessment Questionnaire (MOAQ; Cammann, Fichman, Jenkins, & Kelsh, 1983) and the related instruments in the Michigan Quality of Work Program (Seashore, Lawler, Mirvis, & Cammann, 1983). These instruments were often used in research and served as models for many subsequent instruments. MOAQ includes seven modules that cover individual performance (based on self-reported effort at work) and QWL outcomes (including job satisfaction). Also included in measures of individual responses to the job are intentions and opportunities to leave the organization or job. Other scales cover characteristics of jobs, roles, and tasks; identification with work and the organization; adequacy of training and skills; perceived determinants of pay and importance of various types of rewards; and several facets of supervisory behavior. There are also measures of some group characteristics and processes, including diversity, goal clarity, cohesiveness, involvement in decision making, fragmentation, and openness of communications.

To create a more comprehensive diagnostic instrument, practitioners can supplement data from MOAQ and other studies based on individual perceptions with more behavioral data on individual working conditions and outputs (Higgs & Ashworth, 1996). Data can also be gathered on additional facets of group performance, such as output quantity and quality, goal attainment, innovativeness, efficiency, morale, and reputation for excellence. The Organizational Assessment Inventory (OAI; Van de Ven & Ferry, 1980) provides scales in these areas, as well measures of group diversity and group processes, including conflict management, and normative pressures. Structural features assessed by OAI include control systems, job standardization, role relations, work and unit interdependencies, work flows, and authority distribution. OAI contains separate questionnaires for supervisors and group members so that comparisons of their attitudes and reports can be made. Other instruments within OAI assess divisional (interdepartmental) and organization-level phenomena. Additional factors, such as group or organizational norms and culture, can be assessed with the aid of instruments such as those described in Appendix B.

To obtain data on group-level phenomena from questionnaires such as MOAQ and OAI, the responses from members of a particular work group or administrative unit are averaged to create group scores. For these averages to be meaningful and useful in analysis and feedback, the questionnaires must specify clearly which work groups and supervisors are referred to.

Advantages and Drawbacks of Standardized Questionnaires

Instruments such as MOAQ and OAI contain ready-to-use scales that usually produce valid and reliable measures for many organizational settings. In keeping with current research and organizational theory, these instruments reflect the assumption that there is no one best way to organize groups or organizations. Instead, the optimal combination of system traits is assumed to depend on many variables, including environmental conditions, tasks, technology, personnel, history, and size of the organization.

Despite their appeal, standardized diagnostic instruments also have serious weaknesses and drawbacks. First, they may give practitioners a false sense of confidence that all the factors relevant to a particular client organization have been covered adequately. Second, standard questions are necessarily abstract; hence, they may not be fully applicable to a particular organization or situation. For example, a typical questionnaire item in MOAQ asks respondents to indicate their degree of agreement with the statement, "My supervisor encourages subordinates to participate in making important decisions" (Cammann et al., 1983, p. 108). The responses to this general statement, however, may mask the fact that the supervisor encourages participation in decisions in one area, such as work scheduling, while making decisions alone in other areas, such as budgeting. To obtain data on such situational variations, investigators must determine the situations across which there may be broad variations and write questions about these situations (Enz, 1989; Moch, Cammann, & Cooke, 1983, pp. 199–200).

Third, as in any questionnaire, even apparently simple questions may contain concepts or phrases that may be understood in different ways. For instance, when reacting to the statement, "I get to do a number of different things on my job" (Cammann et al., 1983, p. 94), one person might view diversity in physical actions (e.g., snipping vs. scraping) or minor changes in the tools needed for the job, whereas another would consider all of these operations as "doing the same thing." Fourth, questionnaires are especially vulnerable to biases stemming from the respondent's desire to give socially acceptable answers or to avoid sensitive issues. There may also be tendencies to give artificially consistent responses (Salancik & Pfeffer, 1977; but cf. Stone, 1992). Some instruments include questions designed to detect or minimize biases, whereas others may heighten the risk of bias by phrasing all questions in a single direction.

Observations

Observations can help consultants obtain an idea of the actual behavior and processes that occur within an organization and the ways that members view their work and the organization as a whole. Direct observation can also provide practitioners with data that are more independent of people's interpretations and viewpoints than are responses to questionnaires and interviews. People are often not very good observers of the actions occurring within their groups. Often, they cannot describe group norms, beliefs, and informal behavior patterns or are reluctant to do so. Because observation is time-consuming and requires keen skills, it is often reserved for the analysis of top management groups, whose decisions and solutions to problems are critical to the organization as a whole.

Meetings make an ideal focus for observations. Managers and professionals spend much of their time in meetings, and meeting outcomes form an important part of managerial outputs. Moreover, participants often find meetings to be frustrating and nonproductive. Hence, they may be interested in having consultants help them improve the effectiveness of their meetings.

Observational Techniques

Consultants can structure observations in terms of a general accounting scheme (see Appendix C; Perkins, Nadler, & Hanlon, 1981) or predefined categories for coding observed behavior (Weick, 1985). Experienced practitioners may also conduct unstructured observations to remain open to unanticipated phenomena.

Unless observers use a highly structured coding scheme, they briefly record the observed behavior of the participants using descriptive, nonevaluative language. For example

- Chairperson shouts for order.
- Workers consult each other over how to get the machine going again.
- Nurses are quiet, do not participate in the discussion of the case.

Notations on observed behavior such as these provide the basis for subsequent inferences about group functioning. For example, repeated observations of workers helping each other handle operational snags may lead consultants to conclude that relations between workers are cooperative and facilitate independence from supervisors and technicians. Including such concrete descriptions of behavior will also make feedback more useful to group members. If the practitioners have used a list of topics to guide their observations, they can summarize their findings for each topic and add illustrative descriptions from their notes.

Before beginning observations of a particular setting, investigators often try to learn as much as possible through interviews or informal conversations about the backgrounds of the people to be observed, their roles, the nature of the task facing the group, and the ways that this task or similar ones have been handled in the past. If taking notes during the observation will disturb group members, observers can write their notes as soon as possible after the observation. With practice, observers can recall entire conversations or discussions and record them after completing the observation. Things that the observer did not understand can be clarified through repeated observations or discussions with participants. Additional observations of the group under differing circumstances and repeated observations of similar events will help the observer distinguish between recurring and one-time phenomena. After a clear picture has emerged, results can be compared to those obtained from other data sources and prepared for analysis and feedback.

Analysis

Analysis of diagnostic data can draw on the logical and statistical procedures used in nonapplied research (Hoyle, Harris, & Judd, 2001; Trochim, 2001). Once summarized, nonstatistical data can be analyzed with the help of diagrams such as Figures 3.1 and 3.2. The main findings about each of the categories shown could be recorded on an enlarged version of the figures. The arrows between the boxes could be labeled to describe important system interactions. For example, a summary based on Figure 3.1 might display a link between the tasks of clerical workers (limited authority and access to information) and their job orientations (boredom and alienation). Beneath the figure, supporting evidence of the relation could be recorded, such as the observation that clerical employees who were given more responsibility and information showed higher motivation and less boredom.

An alternative approach is to create a visual model that summarizes the links between sources of ineffectiveness and ineffective outcomes of greatest concern to clients. A similar approach can be used to map the forces most likely to help groups or the organization as a whole face a major challenge, such as attainment of dramatic improvements in client satisfaction or service quality.

If the study includes standard, quantifiable measures of effectiveness and its predictor variables and if data are available for a set of organizations, consultants can benchmark the client organization against the baseline data. More frequently, practitioners make statistical or qualitative comparisons of units within a single organization. They then prepare the data for feedback to group members or plan further study of groups with unusually high or low scores. If data available at the start of a diagnosis suggest that some units are outstanding on important features or are particularly problematic, consultants may focus much of their investigation on these units.

Before undertaking extended multivariate analyses of questionnaire data, practitioners should decide how heavily their diagnosis will rely on these analyses. Alternatively, they could use other methods to gather additional information or provide members of the client group with the major single or bivariate distributions and encourage them to try to account for the findings from their understandings of the organization. Whatever approach is chosen, the data should be presented in an appealing and easy-to-understand form. Reports and trade literature that circulate in a client organization may suggest appropriate formats for presenting data.

Feedback

Procedures

Wide variations exist in procedures for providing feedback from diagnostic studies (Cummings & Worley, 2001, pp. 130–141; Nadler, 1977). Practitioners may give feedback only to the client or clients who called for the study. More frequently, where feedback encourages group problem solving, consultants present their results to all participants in the study or to everyone affected by its findings. Consultants can give feedback to supervisors and subordinates in an organizational unit separately or simultaneously. A danger in providing feedback simultaneously is that supervisors often experience conflicts between receiving criticism and being expected to lead a discussion about planning appropriate action. An alternative design involves providing feedback to task forces or other temporary groups that cut across departmental and hierarchical lines. These groups are assigned responsibility for planning the organization's response to the findings.

In client-focused diagnoses in organization development consultations, consultants usually try to collaborate with members of the client organization to interpret the findings and decide how to deal with them (Burke, 1982, p. 162).

First, the consultant presents a summary of the data and a preliminary analysis. A discussion usually follows in which consultant and participants clarify the findings. Then, the practitioner and group members discuss the implications of the data for action.

Feedback Characteristics

Whatever form feedback takes, people are more likely to accept and act on feedback that has the following characteristics (Block, 1981; Cummings & Worley, 2001, pp. 130–133):

- Relevant and understandable to members
- Descriptive rather than evaluative
- Clear and specific—referring to concrete behavior and situations, illustrating generalizations
- Comparative, including comparisons to similar units or organizations
- Timely—given soon after data gathering
- Believable—providing information about the validity of the data
- Sensitive to members' feelings and motivations rather than provoking anger, defensiveness, or feelings of helplessness
- Limited rather than overwhelming
- Practical and feasible—pointing to issues that members can do something about
- Unfinalized—leaving room for members to contribute to data analysis and make their own decisions about implications for actions

Even if practitioners cannot meet these exacting standards completely, they can improve their effectiveness by changing their feedback procedures so that they are closer to these ideals.

EXERCISES

1. Using Questionnaires to Diagnose Group Processes

Choose two work groups or units on which background information is available. These groups should perform similar tasks and have similar types of employees. Try to locate one group reputed to have positive features (e.g., high work quality or positive staff relations) and another that seems weak in the same areas. Develop a questionnaire on key aspects of group process with approximately 10 questions drawn from one or more of the standardized questionnaires discussed in this chapter and Appendix B. Distribute the questionnaire to members of both groups after you have explained that the data will be used only for an exercise and will not be distributed to anyone outside of the groups. Prepare a summary of the average responses to each question for the two groups and compare your results to the previous information you had on the groups. If the results differ from your expectations, try to account for these differences. Explain how you would give feedback to the supervisors and members of both groups to facilitate constructive discussion and problem solving. If requested, prepare a separate summary of the findings for each group.

2. Observing Meetings

Discuss problems or challenges facing a group with one of its leading members. Choose features of group behavior, processes, and culture discussed in this chapter or listed in Appendix C that might be related to these problems or challenges and can be readily observed during group meetings. Observe at least two meetings of the group. Write a report on the following topics:

1. Background on the group and the meetings (type of meetings, purpose, and circumstances; e.g., weekly staff meeting or ad hoc session), participants, and organizational context
2. Summary of observations of the selected features
3. Criteria for evaluating group effectiveness
4. Sources of effectiveness and ineffectiveness
5. Nature of presented problems or challenges and possible ways to address them
6. Additional ways to improve effectiveness or reduce ineffectiveness
7. Procedure for providing feedback to participants

3. Assessing Human Resource Management Programs

Choose one HRM function, such as staff development, from the lists in this chapter. Interview the manager who has the most direct responsibility for administering operations in this area, such as the director of personnel. Ask this person to define the organization's needs and activities in this functional area in terms of the desired individual and group characteristics or outcomes. Ask what standards are currently used to assess whether these needs are being met and whether any internal or external developments require redefinitions of these needs and standards. Based on this interview, write a proposal to diagnose the extent to which current HRM programs, such as on-the-job-training, meet current and anticipated needs. Be specific about the units of analysis, the kinds of data to be gathered, and the types of inferences you will make from these data.

NOTES

1. Following current usage, the terms *group* and *team* are used interchangeably.
2. Figure 3.1 and the following discussion draw in part on Lawler, Nadler, and Mirvis (1983, pp. 20–25); see Harrison and Shirom (1999, pp. 145–165) for further discussion of this model and references to the research literature.
3. This case derives from a report by Adler and Bartholomew (1992) of a study of human resource programs in 50 North American firms.
4. This presentation of the model reflects both the work of Hackman and colleagues and a modification and critique in Harrison and Shirom (1999, pp. 166–173).
5. See Appendix B in this volume for an instrument development by Hackman and colleagues.
6. In anthropological studies, such individuals are called *informants,* a term that cannot be used in diagnosis because of its negative connotations.

4

System Fits and Organizational Politics

In this chapter, the open systems model is used as a guide for assessing fits among system components and fits between current system features and organizational goals and strategies. Emphasis is placed on assessing fits among organization design features that managers can influence. Gaps between emergent behavior and official mandates and objectives are also discussed. The final section of the chapter treats organizational power and politics, which are crucial emergent features of organizational life.

This chapter shows how to use the open systems model to uncover organizational conditions that can undermine or enhance effectiveness in entire divisions or organizations. To apply the system model, practitioners of diagnosis assess the degree of fit among system components and the impact of current fits. *Fit* (also called *alignment* and *congruence*) refers to the extent to which the behavioral or organizational requirements and constraints in one part of a system are compatible with those in other parts.

Macrolevel system features, such as those discussed in this chapter, often create "latent conditions" (Reason, 1997), which influence the more visible micropractices of individuals and work groups. People who are used to dealing with problems in terms of individual motivation, effort, and interpersonal relations may not always see the connections between such symptoms and underlying macrolevel conditions. Poor alignment among macro conditions, however, can lead to many unsatisfactory individual, interpersonal, and group outcomes. Here are problems that are often blamed on individuals but may reflect poor fit among broad organizational features:

- Errors, accidents, and other quality deficiencies
- High levels of absenteeism and turnover
- Unsatisfactory customer-client relations
- Bitter, enduring conflicts between units
- Tasks being neglected or falling between the cracks
- Communication delays and failures
- Lack of innovation or creativity

Macrolevel forces and alignments can also contribute to problems and challenges that managers sometimes attribute to external causes that lie beyond their control. Examples of such major problems include the following:

- Stagnant or declining sales and revenues
- Loss of public support or confidence
- Trailing behind competitors and industry standards
- Inability to recruit top candidates for jobs
- Failures of joint ventures and mergers
- Difficulties implementing plans and programs

DIAGNOSING SYSTEM FITS

If consultants adopt a focused approach to diagnosis, such as the sharp-image approach described in Chapter 1, they examine fits that are directly related to problems or challenges presented by clients or discovered during entry or early data gathering. It is also possible to assess fits related to system features that clients plan to redesign. For instance, clients may ask for help in planning mergers with another firm or reengineering work processes. In other instances, clients ask for help from consultants only when difficulties arise during implementation of projects, programs, and technologies.[1]

Practitioners who want to conduct a comprehensive diagnostic study can make preliminary assessments of fits among system components and fits between the current system and a future one as envisioned in organizational plans and strategies. This approach is particularly useful when consultants assess the contribution of system fits to competitive advantage (Porter, 1996) or when fundamental, strategic changes are occurring in system components, such as structure, technology, and environment. Such changes sometimes weaken organizational performance (Ramanujam, 2003) and give rise to misalignments among components. Another possibility is to examine fits among different system levels—for example, individual-group, individual-organization, and group-organization fits (Nadler & Tushman, 1980).

The following case (Beckhard & Harris, 1975, p. 52) illustrates how poor fit between managerial processes (goal formation and leadership) and reward systems (structures and processes) at the divisional level can affect motivation and individual behavior.

Case 7

The head of a major corporate division was frustrated by his subordinates' lack of motivation to work with him in planning for the future of the business and their lack of attention to developing the managerial potential of their subordinates. Repeated exhortations about these matters produced few results, although the division managers agreed that change was desirable. The barrier to change was that there were no meaningful rewards for engaging in planning or management development and no punishments for not doing so. Moreover, managers were directly accountable for short-term profits in their divisions. If they failed to show a profit, they would be fired on the spot.

The division head defined involvement in planning and management development as divisional objectives, but the division's reward and control procedures led managers to strive exclusively for more tangible, short-term results. Misfits such as these can stem from inertia and lack of attention to achieving system congruity, bureaucratic pressures, and conflicts among the many external and internal constraints to which management is subject (Gresov, 1989).

Figure 4.1 provides a schematic summary of the steps required to diagnose fits. The step in the figure labeled "choose fits" is treated in the following section. The next two steps in the figure are addressed in the sections Ways to Assess Fits, Diagnosing Organization Design, and Emergent Behavior and Culture Versus Official Mandates. The step labeled "assess impacts" is discussed in Assessing the Impacts of Fits and Gaps.

The Choice of Fits

Starting With Client Problems

When starting from presented problems and challenges, practitioners hunt for related, underlying conditions that have a wider impact on organizational effectiveness. By reporting these underlying conditions, the practitioner may help clients solve the original problems, reduce other signs of ineffectiveness, and enhance overall organizational effectiveness.

For example, a practitioner who encounters complaints about tasks being neglected or handled poorly can examine links between structure and two critical processes: decision making and communication. Responsibility charting, a procedure used in many large corporations (Galbraith, 1977, p. 171), provides one way to clarify these links. First, during interviews or workshops the practitioner asks group members to list key tasks or decision areas. In a project group, these might include budgeting, scheduling, allocating personnel, and changing design specifications of a product. Second, each member is asked to list the

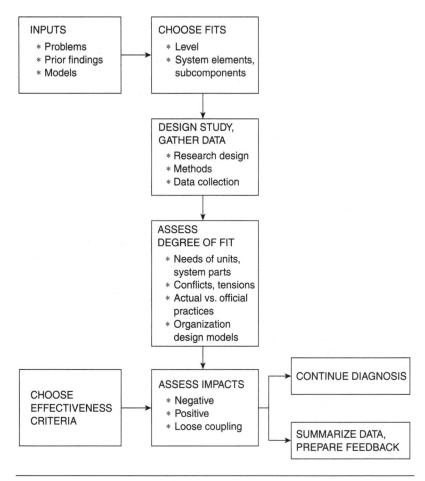

Figure 4.1   Diagnosing System Fits

positions that might be involved in these areas (e.g., project director, general manager, and laboratory manager); indicate who is assigned responsibility for performing tasks; and note who is supposed to approve the work, be consulted, and be informed. The data usually reveal ambiguities relating to one or more task areas. Consultants can use these data as feedback to stimulate efforts to redefine responsibilities and clarify relations. Feedback can also lead clients and consultants to evaluate fundamental organizational features, such as delegation of authority, coordination mechanisms, and the division of labor. For instance, discussion of approval procedures for work scheduling might reveal that many minor scheduling changes are needed, and that scheduling would operate more smoothly if middle-level managers received authority to make such minor changes and inform the project head afterward.

Using a Checklist of Important Fits

When practitioners aim for a more comprehensive diagnosis, they may use a checklist such as the one shown in Table 4.1 as an aid to fit assessment. This table presents fits that research and practice have shown to be especially important (Daft, 2004; Harrison & Shirom, 1999; Meyer, Tsui, & Hinnings, 1993; Van de Ven & Drazin, 1985). After a preliminary assessment of major fits, practitioners can concentrate on instances of poor alignment or areas in which change is likely to disrupt current alignments. The system features of divisions within large and complex organizations will probably differ substantially from one another. Hence, it is best to begin by examining fits within divisions. If necessary, fits within the total organization can be considered subsequently.

Ways to Assess Fits

One practical way to assess fits is to examine the compatibility of requirements, needs, or procedures in different units or system parts. Fits among units are weak if the work of one unit is disrupted because of inadequate inputs from another unit or poor synchronization with other units. For example, hospital emergency departments sometimes experience overcrowding because inpatient units encounter difficulties discharging patients and the housekeeping unit does not quickly prepare beds when they are vacated.

A second way to assess fit is to investigate whether participants feel subject to conflicting expectations or pressures and check whether these conflicts are the result of poor fit. In Case 7, for example, a department manager might have complained during an interview, "My boss wants me to work on management development, but if I do, I'll be in hot water when he goes over my quarterly sales results!" The practitioner would then check whether other managers made similar comments and whether rewards were closely tied to quarterly performance while ignoring management development activities. A third possibility is to assess whether system components or subcomponents fit together in ways that organizational research suggests they should.

Diagnosing Organization Design

Consultants to management often concentrate their diagnoses on fits involving design tools—organizational arrangements that can most readily be redesigned

(Text continued on page 85)

Table 4.1
Questions About Fits

Focal Area	Fit With
Environment	*Internal System*[a] Does the environment provide access to resources (funds, services, information, and people) needed for smooth operations? Are changes in the environment likely to disrupt resource flows? Is demand low or uncertain for some products and services (outputs)? Is demand changing? Do outputs meet the expectations of customers and other external stakeholders?
Human Resources	*System Processing (Behavior, Processes, and Technology) and Structure* Do employees' skills and training fit their job requirements and equip them to handle new tasks and technologies? Are the best people attracted and retained by the current reward system and opportunities for advancement? Are professionals and others seeking autonomy and challenge assigned to less structured and less tightly controlled jobs? *Goals and Strategies* Do employees' skills and knowledge support managerial goals and strategies?
Goals and Strategies	*Environment* Are products and services directed to the appropriate environmental niches? Are there other unexploited markets and environments? Do current strategies help identify and sustain competitive advantage? *Resources* Can current and planned strategies and programs be supported by available resources? Can current capacities and resources be stretched to support strategies? *Behavior and Processes, Culture* Are plans for change compatible with current norms, values, behavior, and beliefs?

a. Internal system includes all system components except environment.

Focal Area	Fit With
Technology	*Environment*
	How up to date are current technologies?
	Do technologies meet industry and sector standards? Do they fulfill the expectations of suppliers, clients, and customers?
	Do managers use technologies to gain and maintain market share?
	Behavior and Processes
	How fully are the capabilities of new technologies used?
	Do technologies sustain collaboration within cross-functional teams and among work groups and larger units?
	Are technologies used appropriately to reduce errors, solve quality problems, and deal with other forms of ineffectiveness?
	Structure
	Are technologies compatible among organizations (or units) that exchange products and information or engage in strategic alliances?
	Culture
	Are current and proposed technologies compatible with prevailing practices, values, norms, and beliefs within the organization and in subgroups responsible for technology implementation?
Internal System	*Environment*
	How compatible are structures, behavior, and culture with those of partners in mergers and strategic alliances?
	How well do current administrative practices bridge between members of the organization and customers, clients, and external partners?
Structure	*Technology, Behavior and Processes, and Environment*
	Are people who need to work together grouped in units or linked by appropriate coordinating mechanisms?
	Are divisions and subunits large enough to attain efficiencies in routine tasks but small enough to allow for rapid communication and response to external change?

(Continued)

Table 4.1 (Continued)

Focal Area	Fit With
	Are divisions diverse enough in their prevailing practices to allow for effective response to divergent environments and tasks? Are there effective mechanisms for integrating work across divisions?
	Are people who perform divergent functions or work in separate units divided by bitter conflicts or power struggles?
	Are there tasks or functions that no one does adequately and others for which there are unjustified overlaps among people or units?
	Are arrangements for coordinating work and information flows appropriate to tasks, technology, and environment?
	Have administrative processes been redesigned to take full advantage of new technical systems?
	Are authority and responsibility located as far down as feasible in the hierarchy?
	Do people and units have enough power and resources to accomplish their tasks adequately? Do they have the capacity to innovate and improve the organization?
	Do physical and geographic layouts contribute to the flow of work and information?
	Human Resources
	How well do work arrangements, human resource development, and benefits meet the needs of diverse groups of employees, including single parents, older employees, those with physical disabilities, and people whose native language differs from the dominant one?
Behavior and Processes	*Culture*
	Do top and middle managers foster a sense of mission and identity among members?
	Environment
	Do managers and employees successfully project the organizational identity to external stakeholders?

by their clients (Beer, 1980, p. 27; Daft, 2004; Mintzberg, 1979). Managers use design tools to structure the options available to their staff and create pressures to act in a particular manner. For example, the division head in Case 7 was able to recalculate bonus pay so as to reflect contributions to planning and management development. This design change helped solve the initial problem. The greater the authority and autonomy of clients, the more readily they can make changes in design factors. Collective bargaining agreements, government regulations, and internal opposition may severely constrain the design options available to both public- and private-sector managers.

Design tools to consider during diagnosis include the following:

- Contractual arrangements, network ties, and strategic alliances (mergers and joint ventures) with other organizations
- Structural grouping of positions and units
- Positions and procedures that monitor the environment
- Job designs
- Human resource programs
- Management information systems
- Mechanisms for coordinating internal and external relations among units or positions
- Procedures for monitoring, evaluating, and rewarding performance
- Performance control and quality assurance procedures
- Accounting and budgeting systems
- Geographic location and physical layout
- Communication channels (including bottom-up and organization-environment communications)

The following discussion illustrates the importance of design tools such as these and reviews important design issues that arise at the interorganizational, organizational, and divisional levels.

Alliances Among Organizations

An increasing number of organizations are forging ties with other organizations. These may be contractual links and other specialized forms of cooperation; more enduring and broader network collaborations; or strategic alliances, including joint ventures and partial ownership arrangements. Diagnosis of current interorganizational ties and assessment of proposed linkages can examine fits between organizations and fits among their system subcomponents (Bluedorn & Lundgren, 1993). In general, the greater the proposed integration of management procedures and cultures, the greater the need for system fit between partners (Osborn & Baughn, 1993). Strategic alliances pose two diagnostic issues: First, how good is the fit between the partners' management procedures and cultures? Second, if fit is poor, do the managers within one of the organizations have the ability and desire to change their organization to achieve fit (Cartwright & Cooper, 1993)?

To address these diagnostic issues, practitioners can interview or survey people involved in a merger or strategic alliance. The practitioner would examine the alliance's anticipated or current impact on administrative practices, the image and culture of the organizations, and the staff of both organizations (Buono & Bowditch, 1989). Feedback from the groups affected by a merger or strategic alliance can help top management plan steps that will facilitate the alliance and deal with the plurality of needs, cultural orientations, and interests among the participants in the new venture. To facilitate management or planning of design changes, practitioners can also conduct workshops in which clients review systematically the benefits they seek to achieve by proposed or current alliances and likely risks and costs of such alliances.

Links Between Divisions

In large organizations, operating difficulties often revolve around relations between operating divisions. To examine these relations in complex organizations with semiautonomous divisions, practitioners can treat the divisions like organizations in a network and pose questions that are analogous to questions about interorganizational relations.[2] Working relations for each focal division can be thought of as involving exchanges of products, services, and resources. The practitioner then traces the exchanges between the focal division and corporate headquarters, between the division and other parts of the corporation (the corporate environment), and between the division and external organizations and markets. This network approach to multidivisional organizations allows examination of the benefits and drawbacks for each division of current structures and management processes, such as the mechanisms used by corporate headquarters to monitor and evaluate division performance. Viewing multidivisional firms in this way also helps practitioners identify forces facilitating and blocking cooperation across divisional boundaries, including the boundary between corporate headquarters and each division.

Network measurement and modeling techniques (Nelson, 1988; Scott, 2000) enable practitioners to gather quantitative data on such intraorganizational relations and allow for comparisons between current relations between divisions and desired ones (Nelson & Mathews, 1991). Another assessment technique uses questionnaires to ask people in boundary-spanning roles to report on the content and quality of their exchanges with members of units in and outside the organization (Van de Ven & Ferry, 1980).

Mechanistic Versus Organic Systems

This well-known typology provides a basis for assessing how well organizational or divisional management systems (i.e., structures, processes, and culture) are aligned with their environments, tasks, and technologies (Harrison & Shirom, 1999, pp. 205–207; Tichy, 1983). A long research tradition indicates that organic systems are more able to adjust rapidly to environmental and technological uncertainties than are mechanistic (i.e., bureaucratic) ones. Organic systems have more diffuse and flexible definitions of roles and responsibilities than do mechanistic systems, are more decentralized, and rely more on lateral coordination mechanisms, which allow for cross-functional coordination and reciprocal interdependencies among actors. Organic systems treat plans more flexibly, change goals and objectives more often, and use more participative forms of decision making than do mechanistic ones. Together, these structural and administrative features give organic systems greater information-processing capacity and help them sustain higher levels of creativity and innovation than mechanistic systems. Organic systems are more costly and more difficult to manage, however. Hence, when the main tasks are routine—high in volume and low in variance—mechanistic systems are usually more efficient and productive than organic ones.

A division or organization may need a more organic management system if it is unable to cope with one or more of the following types of challenges:

- Adapt quickly to change in task environments (e.g., fashion trends) and respond rapidly and decisively to threats and opportunities
- Handle nonroutine tasks in innovative and creative ways
- Meet employee expectations for creative, challenging work
- Coordinate complex relations with other units and organizations

Unless staff development, intrinsic motivation, and employee satisfaction are critical, divisions that use organic arrangements to deal with predictable environments, limited external dependencies, and routine tasks probably fail to take advantage of efficiencies that could be obtained by introducing more mechanistic procedures. If a preliminary application of this model suggests that change is needed in either direction, practitioners can focus more closely on the design tools that clients can most easily use as levers for change.

Hierarchical Versus Lateral Ties

Increasingly, managers and their consultants face choices between designs based on traditional, hierarchical forms of coordination and control and designs based on lateral coordination across organizational boundaries. Lateral ties span administrative boundaries to link people (including customers) who must cooperate to produce a successful product or service. To choose among competing designs and assess the fit of existing designs, practitioners need models that specify uses and possible effects of alternative design principles. One design model (Galbraith, 1977; Tichy, 1983; Tushman & Nadler, 1978), which can contribute to diagnosis of entire organizations, divisions, or smaller units, examines the capacity of organizational arrangements to coordinate three types of interdependencies. First are *pooled interdependencies,* in which units can work independently of each other (e.g., crews in a home construction firm). According to the model, rules and standard operating procedures usually provide adequate coordination of work based on pooled interdependency. Second are *sequential interdependencies,* in which work must flow from one unit to another according to a fixed order and schedule, as it does in assembly-line production. To coordinate this type of work, rules and procedures must be supplemented by detailed planning of relations between units, close monitoring of unit outputs, and supervision from above. Professional and technical training of staff members can also help ensure uniformity of pooled or sequential operations (Mintzberg, 1979).

Where *reciprocal interdependencies* prevail, units or individuals must directly adjust to one other. For example, a television advertising campaign requires close coordination and mutual adjustment among clients, the campaign head, and specialists in design, marketing, and production.

Lateral coordination mechanisms, rather than rules and hierarchies, allow for such two-way communication and mutual adjustment and thereby help people handle diverse, interdependent, uncertain, and rapidly changing tasks.[3] The need for lateral coordination also increases as organizations seek to perform tasks faster and conduct business processes through an intranet (e.g., customer relations management in banks) or via the Internet (e.g., purchasing and stocking inventory). The following list ranks *lateral mechanisms* from the least to the most complex:

1. Voluntary and informal groups, networks, and linking roles
2. E-coordination (e-mail and intranet) across departments
3. Formal (temporary) committees, teams, and project
4. Integrators to lead formal groups
5. Matrix organization

Formal cross-functional teams supplement existing departmental structures without replacing them. Integrator roles, such as project manager or public health coordinator for a municipality, place direct responsibility on the incumbent to coordinate all the functions that contribute to a particular product, service, or process. Matrix structures combine functional and project authority lines in an attempt to cope with uncertain environments and tasks and obtain the advantages of both forms of organization.

Managers often introduce lateral mechanisms to coordinate the diverse activities associated with producing a particular product or service and overcome communication barriers between specialized units or tasks. Despite their potential benefits, complex lateral mechanisms are costly and difficult to administer. The dual-reporting relations that characterize matrix structures, integrator roles, and cross-functional teams create ambiguity and stress for employees and complicate the processes of evaluating and rewarding performance. The expansion of communication channels in these complex structures can create too much information, while overlapping responsibilities produce turf battles and loss of accountability (Bartlett & Ghoshal, 1990; Davis, Lawrence, Kolodny, & Beer, 1977). Cross-functional teamwork creates many tensions for members because they suddenly must renegotiate task definitions and responsibilities, group identities and boundaries, and personal payoffs and costs. Team members who are accustomed to dealing with problems mainly from a narrow, technical point of view or are used to traditional reporting relations may find it difficult to cope with these challenges.

Before recommending restructuring to enhance lateral coordination, consultants and managers would be well advised to consider ways to attain their objectives through simpler mechanisms, such as informal network ties or the rotation of personnel through roles (Galbraith et al., 1993, p. 117). Managers and consultants can also search for ways to increase subunit autonomy and thereby reduce the need for cross-functional ties.

Diagnosis of current coordination designs can be guided by the model of work interdependencies presented previously. In such a diagnosis, people familiar with the work process describe what has to be done to accomplish the work and describe the mechanisms for coordinating and controlling the work process. The practitioner then uses the model to assess the fit between coordination mechanisms and interdependencies and guide inquiry into ways to reduce misfits. A risk in this theory-guided approach to diagnosis is its reliance on generalizations about the work process.

Instead, it is often preferable to inquire more directly about the flow of work and information between units (Rashford & Coghlan, 1994, p. 25; Van de Ven & Ferry, 1980) or even directly observe these interactions. In such a diagnosis, consultants use focus groups, interviews, or questionnaires to examine the nature of the work and the mechanisms used to coordinate and control work processes. Then, signs of ineffectiveness can be traced to underlying causes. Interunit coordination is ineffective if members view coordination procedures as clumsy or inadequate, or if interunit contacts are characterized by frequent interruptions, misunderstandings, surprises, and high levels of conflict. If these problems are common, members may not be using existing coordinating mechanisms adequately, or the coordination mechanisms may be inappropriate.

Centralization Versus Decentralization

A design issue that arises at almost all organizational levels concerns the degree of centralization. When power and authority are highly centralized, control over important resources and decisions is concentrated at higher ranks. Shifting toward a more decentralized distribution of authority and power may lead to the following advantages:

- Reduced burden on top management to make decisions and process information
- Cost savings from reduction in administrative levels and paperwork
- Improved information flow and decision quality
- Flexible and rapid response to local conditions
- Improved morale
- More innovation
- More responsibility for results among lower ranks
- Enhanced ability of middle managers to solve problems on their own
- Better management development

Decentralization can also produce disadvantages, however, including the following:

- Reduction in top management's ability to forge a unifying strategy and respond quickly to change
- Increased costs for training, compensation, capital equipment, and plant
- Duplication of positions
- Creation of local power centers
- Heightened conflict between units

To diagnose the existing distribution of authority and power, practitioners examine the level at which people are authorized to make decisions in key functional areas and, if possible, actual patterns of decision making and power distribution. After the practitioner has characterized the current degree of decentralization within the focal unit, possible costs and benefits of changes in this pattern can be considered in light of the managers' and the consultants' knowledge of the organization and in light of explicit effectiveness criteria.

Combining Opposing Design Principles

Increasingly, consultants and researchers find that organizations can prosper by simultaneously pursuing what at first appear to be opposing design principles (Brown & Eisenhardt, 1997; Cameron & Quinn, 1988). Instead of choosing between alternatives such as centralization versus decentralization, rigid versus flexible structures, or hierarchical versus lateral coordination, managers may be able to find ways to enjoy simultaneously some of the payoffs of both alternatives.

To help decision makers discover such possibilities and avoid controversial and costly restructurings, practitioners can search for the simplest designs that provide adequate lateral coordination. Managers can then incorporate these lateral mechanisms into existing hierarchical structures. For example, "mirror-image" structures make cross-functional ties easier without abandoning functional departments or creating complicated dual-reporting arrangements (Galbraith et al., 1993, pp. 48–49). In this structure, each functional unit is subdivided into an identical set of product or commodity groups. For instance, a public welfare organization could create units within its functional groups that dealt with parallel client groups, such as retirement-age clients, single parents, and adolescents. Such an arrangement helps people working within separate functional groups locate their counterparts in other units who serve the same clients, contribute to the same service, or work on the same product. Another incremental change that can enhance coordination adds responsibility for processes such as customer service or product development onto managers' existing responsibilities (Davenport, 1993, pp. 161–162).

Information technologies also offer top management the opportunity to take advantage of decentralization without abandoning centralized control (Keen, 1990). Today's information systems allow managers of large firms or divisions to monitor practices and performance of subordinate units while at the same time giving them the authority, resources, and feedback needed to make decisions autonomously. In other words, instead of striving for design consistency, practitioners and their clients can benefit by combining multiple and even opposing design principles. By doing so, they can sometimes develop arrangements that best fit the changing functional needs of the organization and respond effectively to the expectations of multiple stakeholders.

EMERGENT BEHAVIOR AND
CULTURE VERSUS OFFICIAL MANDATES

Gap Analysis

Another way to uncover sources of ineffectiveness and motivate desire for change is to provide feedback on gaps (or lack of fit) between officially mandated behavior and emergent behavior and culture.[4] Actual practices, norms, and beliefs emerge through interactions among the people who set objectives, make plans, and give orders and the people who carry them out in practice. The negotiations that shape emergent behavior and organizational culture often occur in ways that are hidden from the view of consultants and even from many participants (Weick & Quinn, 1999).

Nonetheless, through careful investigation practitioners can often find gaps between official mandates and the following types of emergent behavior and culture:

- Operative goals and priorities
- Working definitions of roles and functional responsibilities
- Actual work techniques and procedures
- Norms and beliefs about official rules of conduct and legal standards
- Informal reward systems, including beliefs and norms about rewards
- Informal leadership
- Personal ties and networks
- Routines for dealing with clients, customers, and outsiders
- Popular practices for influencing peers and superiors

Emergent behavior can diverge greatly from official descriptions of these practices and from official purposes and procedures. Managers, for example, may report that they frequently consult with their subordinates before reaching major decisions, but the subordinates' own reports and other data sources on decision making (e.g., lists of members of powerful committees) may not confirm this idealized picture.

Other key processes, including controlling and rewarding, supervision, decision making, and conflict management, also warrant attention, as do prevailing beliefs and norms (organizational culture) about the organization and its environment. Standards of safety, reliability, or customer service can be undermined by employee beliefs about "what it takes to get ahead" or norms about dealing with customers "who want too much help." Prevailing norms and beliefs—and sometimes actions by senior officials—may encourage shady business practices or unethical or illegal forms of personal conduct, such as sexual harassment. By shaping the kinds of information that members regard as valid and important, shared beliefs also affect the ability of members of an organization to respond to external and internal challenges. For example, instead of striving to improve their firm's position, employees in a financial services firm may become pessimistic about their firm's ability to survey a hostile takeover and decide to seek jobs elsewhere, "before it's too late."

Collecting Data on Emergent Behavior and Culture

Practitioners of diagnosis can enrich their understanding of emergent behavior by triangulating their data-gathering methods using multiple measures, and seeking information from people with divergent roles and viewpoints. Documents and declarations about a firm that are meant for broad distribution can provide useful insights into the image of the firm that the authors seek to project to the public. These statements, however, cannot serve as guides to emergent organizational practices.

The richest data on emergent practices usually come from direct observations, intensive interviews, or analyses of existing organizational records. Data on prevailing practices can also be obtained from instruments such as those reviewed in Appendix B or from open interviews. Data on ongoing social and working relations can also be obtained using sociometric questionnaires. Respondents to these questionnaires name people or positions with whom they work closely or have frequent contact (Brass & Burkhardt, 1993). The patterns of one-way and mutual choice between respondents can then be analyzed to provide maps of relations or simple statistical analyses of network ties (Nelson, 1988). There are also standard questionnaires on beliefs, norms, and values, but these must overcome some serious methodological difficulties (Denison, 1996; Harrison & Shirom, 1999, pp. 263–265).

Open or semistructured interviews elicit the most useful and valid data when respondents provide explicit descriptions of how they act in a range of work situations, rather than giving generalizations or expressing attitudes. To obtain data about the actual division of labor within a project group, for example, a researcher can ask team members to describe what each person did during the design of a project. Then, the researcher draws conclusions after examining patterns and variations across a set of episodes or interviews. This procedure is more likely to yield valid results than asking members to generalize about whether "responsibilities are clear" in the group or asking perceptual questions (e.g., "Are task assignments flexible enough to allow for unforeseen circumstances?").

A useful technique for focusing questions explicitly on behavior is to ask respondents to describe in detail how they dealt with critical incidents—specific episodes that concretely illustrate the type of behavior under study. For example, to study the use and consequences of different types of influence techniques, Schilit and Locke (1982) asked respondents to describe in detail one successful and one unsuccessful attempt to influence their supervisors at work. In a similar vein, investigators seeking information on emergent norms and channels of communication can ask about instances in which subordinates had bad news for their supervisor or for higher-level managers. What, if anything, did subordinates say or do? If they told their supervisors or others higher up in the organization, how did these people deal with the discrediting information (Argyris & Schon, 1995)?

Another fruitful strategy for examining emergent practices is to gather data from interviews and organizational records concerning the whole path along which a service, a product, a client, or an idea moves through an organization. To study hospital coordination mechanisms, for example, investigators can trace the entire course of treatment of representative hospital patients, from reception to completion of treatment (Lynam, Smith, & Dwyer, 1994). To study decision making and working relations in an industrial firm, they can gather retrospective data on the development of a new product from its earliest design stages through routine production.

An advantage of direct observations and analysis of existing data is that much information may be obtained unobtrusively (Webb, Campbell, Schwartz, & Seechrest, 1966), without interfering with people's behavior or influencing it. For example, by observing attendance at meetings or by checking records, practitioners might discover that a project that is officially assigned high priority is being neglected by senior staff members. Although such observational data can be very informative, their reliability may be low, and they are usually difficult to quantify. Unless observations are quite intensive, the data obtained from them usually must be compared to results obtained from other techniques.

ASSESSING THE IMPACTS OF FITS AND GAPS

As Figure 4.1 suggests, consultants should assess the impacts of system fits directly rather than assuming that high levels of fit or system integration are always preferable. Instead, any particular pattern and level of fit, or any gap between emergent practice and official mandates, can be assumed to have both costs and benefits that can be identified and weighed in terms of specific effectiveness criteria. Consider the assessment of gaps between official rules and emergent behavior: The hoarding of supplies by units on a military base probably causes wastage and increases costs, but the practice may also contribute to solidarity and morale within units. In some instances, outright violations of official procedures help employees do better work. For example, champions of new products may violate official directives and procedures by fudging budget entries and diverting resources to new product development (Peters & Waterman, 1982).

Care is required in assessing the impacts of fits and gaps, because many organizations are loosely coupled (Orton & Weick, 1990) so that units or even functions are not closely connected to one another. Such organizations can operate successfully despite fairly high levels of structural incongruity and inconsistency. Divergence in management systems may also reflect the fact that there has been differentiation among divisions, units, or occupational groups, which deal with divergent environments, technologies, or bodies of knowledge. Moreover, inconsistent or ambiguous management systems can foster creativity and innovation. For instance, in pursuit of these ends, universities, some knowledge-intensive firms (Starbuck, 1992), and academic hospitals often tolerate empire building by leading experts, political infighting, and ambiguous definitions of the responsibilities of teams and individuals. If clients and practitioners value innovation and creativity, they would be unwise to try to force system components into overly tight alignment. Judged in terms of their impact on innovativeness and adaptation to change, the fits in many organizations turn out to be too tight rather than too loose (Katz & Kahn, 1978, p. 174).

Finally, in assessing fits and gaps, practitioners should keep in mind that many tasks and organizational needs can be handled in more than one way. Hence, there is room for variation within recurring organizational types, such as organic and mechanistic systems (Van de Ven & Drazin, 1985). For all these reasons, consultants should assess system fits and lack of fits in terms of explicit effectiveness criteria. Then, they can decide whether a lack of fit between certain system components or parts of an organization is detrimental and what steps, if any, should be taken to improve fits.

POWER AND POLITICS

Power distribution and organizational politics, which involves the use of power, are among the most important emergent features in organizations. The terms *power* and *influence* refer to the capacity to get things done, including the ability to get people to do things that they might otherwise not do (Mintzberg, 1983, p. 5).[5] Political actions are attempts by actors or groups of people (stakeholders) to obtain favorable outcomes in areas of importance to them. These actions often seek to influence budgeting decisions and other forms of resource allocation; shape organizational strategies, goals, and programs; promote or resist personnel changes; and resolve conflicts and crises.

Sometimes, political processes and structures become focal points for diagnosis. More often, they help define the setting in which diagnosis and planning for change take place. Understanding the structure and uses of power also helps consultants recognize that their own diagnoses are a form of intervention into the organizational status quo and contain important political implications for members of the client system (see Chapter 6). Diagnoses sometimes produce results that benefit some groups or members while threatening others. In addition, diagnosis often shapes members' expectations concerning organizational change. Suppose, for example, that employees in a firm fear that management plans to downsize. When a consultant is hired to do a diagnostic study, the employees will quite naturally assume that the study will justify cutbacks and perhaps also identify victims.

Politics of Consultation and Change

Even if an understanding of political processes and power distribution does not lead directly to proposals for organizational improvement, it can greatly help consultants manage the consulting process (Greiner & Schein, 1988; Harrison, 1991; Harrison & Shirom, 1999). Diagnosis of politics can also help managers plan more feasible routes to implementing change. In such assessments, information is needed on the stakeholders affected by proposed changes, their orientations toward these changes, and their capacity to support or resist change.

Careful analysis of stakeholders' positions on proposed change sometimes uncovers a way of unfreezing resistance to change. For example, a proposal to introduce a night shift aroused union opposition in an air shipping firm. The union's opposition melted away, however, when it became clear that there were enough employees willing to work nights and staff the third shift (Harrison & Shirom, 1999, pp. 131–132). In other cases, stakeholder analysis will show that stakeholders are not likely to cooperate with a proposed managerial change. In these instances, some modification of the proposal may make it more feasible. Feasibility of change and the appropriateness of intervention techniques also depend on broader social and organizational forces. For example, team building and many other traditional organization development techniques, which require open communication, do not work well in organizations or national cultures that emphasize distinctions of status and authority, nor do these techniques fit settings in which there are fundamental conflicts of interest among subgroups (Cummings & Worley, 2001; Reason, 1984).

Diagnosing the Distribution and Uses of Power

Consultants and their clients need to directly examine organizational consequences of politics. Some organizations are reduced to a state of paralysis by conflicts among powerful internal and external stakeholders. In others, people spend so much time planning and parrying political maneuvers that they have little time and energy left for anything else. Political action, however, can be a force for development and organizational adaptation. Members of an organization can use power to champion changes that will benefit many groups within the organization, along with external stakeholders. For example, in many organizations, proposals for new products and other innovations are accepted only when powerful managers persuade decision makers to provide the resources needed to develop a new idea and then fight to overcome opposition to its implementation (Frost & Egri, 1991).

Practitioners of diagnosis can only evaluate the consequences of political activity from the viewpoints of particular actors within the organization and in terms of specific effectiveness criteria. Consider, for example, a situation in which workers join forces with local politicians in delaying the closing of an unprofitable plant until a joint labor-management committee can draft a reorganization proposal. If a consultant to the management of the firm concentrated solely on finding ways to improve the firm's profitability, the consultant would view the workers' action as harming organizational effectiveness. In contrast, a consultant to the union would probably view the workers' actions favorably, as might a consultant to management who placed greater stress on job security, plant morale, and the standing of the firm in the community.

In addition to evaluating the consequences of politics, diagnosis can assess the effects of the tactics that people use to influence others. People in authority give orders, reward particular actions, set agendas, and define issues for others. Employees lacking authority, as well as those who have it, use appeals to higher authorities, coalition formation, personal connections, selective use of information, threats and sanctions, and informal exchanges and deal making (Porter, Allen, & Angle, 1981; Schilit & Locke, 1982).

To assess the impact of particular influence tactics and other uses of power, practitioners need to consider issues such as these:

- How do those who are subject to a particular influence tactic react to it?
- Does the use of this tactic increase tensions or conflicts between groups?
- Do political deals or appeals to personal connections and loyalties undercut efforts to improve performance and maintain standards of excellence?
- Do the methods used to resolve conflicts produce lasting solutions that are regarded as fair?

Another issue that often arises in diagnosis of managerial structures and processes concerns the degree to which particular groups or people are empowered—in the sense of having sufficient resources, knowledge, skills, and influence to accomplish their tasks. Lack of power can make it difficult for individuals, teams, or entire categories of employees, such as women and minorities, to exercise influence over organizational operations and to get difficult tasks done (Kanter, 1979; Mainero, 1986). Moreover, lack of power can lead employees to do their work mechanistically, resist managerial initiatives, and be less productive than they could be.

To investigate empowerment, practitioners can ask employees about their feelings of competence, self-determination, and ability to have an impact on operational, administrative, and strategic outcomes at work (Spreitzer, 1996; Thomas & Velthouse, 1990). It is also possible to use measures that have been developed for specific types of workers (Bowen & Lawler, 1992). A more behavioral approach examines employee actions during critical incidents. For example, Mainero (1986) asked respondents to describe what they did when they faced frustrating situations in which they found themselves dependent on others at work. It is also possible to examine group or organizational conditions that support empowerment, including delegation of authority and reduction of direct control, access to information and needed resources, normative support, and use of reward and control systems that encourage employee discretion and initiative (Brass & Buckhardt, 1993; Ibarra, 1993; Spreitzer, 1996).

In assessing empowerment, consultants and their clients need to weigh possible costs and benefits in terms of explicit effectiveness criteria, which are relevant to clients and other stakeholders. Empowering first-line service employees, for example, can improve service and quality but may also add to the costs of personnel selection, training, and pay. Furthermore, employees may justly worry that programs empowering them to handle more complicated tasks will lead to more work and responsibility for the same pay and may provide justifications for staff reductions.

Investigating Power and Politics[6]

Gathering trustworthy information on power and influence processes is a challenge to organizational consultants. First, they need to decide which people and groups act or might act in ways that could influence the consulting process or the organizational features being studied. In addition to high-ranking managers, interest groups (stakeholders) may develop along the lines of departments, occupations, ranks, and social characteristics (e.g., gender and ethnic background). Naturally, actors concerned with one issue, such as the reengineering of sales jobs, may be different from those concerned with another, such as budget allocations. After investigators have identified key issues and actors, they can conduct a stakeholder analysis (see Chapter 2 and Exercise 4 at the end of this chapter), charting key actors for each issue, their positions on the issue, coalitions and other links among these actors, their relative power, capacity for action, and likely impacts of these actions.

The sensitivity and informal character of political power and organizational politics make them difficult to observe in action. Hence, consultants and researchers usually search for overt manifestations of power, such as those shown in Table 4.2.

Table 4.2
Who Is Powerful?

Indicators and Guiding Questions	Research Methods
Resources: What kinds of resources are most important to members— funds, equipment, personnel, information, knowledge? Who gets disproportionate shares? In what units or job categories are pay and benefits particularly generous?	Observe and/or interview for key resources and their distribution; examine budget allocations, and salary scales.
Who controls resource acquisition and distribution?	Examine organization charts and job descriptions; ask knowledgeable people.
Centrality: Which technical and administrative processes are vital to everyday operations? Which are critical to success? Who influences and participates in them? Which individuals and groups do people consult for vital information, advice, and help in influencing key decisions?	Interview unit heads, study organization charts, and study job descriptions; analyze reports from interviews or workshops on troubleshooting, crises, failures, and successes; examine network ties through interviews and questionnaires; interview on emergent practices and routines.
Who handles contacts with powerful external organizations and groups? Who holds central positions in important networks?	Interview, examine organization charts; survey unit heads on external contacts and network ties.
Irreplaceability: Who is considered irreplaceable?	Interview knowledgeable members; survey members of relevant units.

(Continued)

Table 4.2 (Continued)

Indicators and Guiding Questions	Research Methods
Structure: Who holds top positions (titles) in the hierarchy? How many titles/roles does each person have? What share of ownership do top people have?	Examine organization charts, reports, and records.
Participation and Influence in Decision Making: Who participates in key official and unofficial forums? Who gets access to top decision makers?	Examine organization charts, job descriptions, and reports on membership in decision-making bodies; observe participation; interview on access and participation.
Whose views dominate major decisions? Who wins in power struggles and conflicts?	Analyze decisions as reported in documents, press, interviews, and workshops.
To whom do members turn for sponsorship of projects, career development?	Analyze personal and project successes and failures reported in interviews, workshops.
Symbols: What are the main symbols of status and power (e.g., titles, and office facilities)? Who displays these symbols?	Observe nature, use, and distribution of status symbols; interview knowledgeable members.
Reputation: Which groups, units, and people are regarded as especially powerful?	Survey members for ranking; interview; observe attention, and deference granted to people and groups.
Which units do people join order get ahead fast? With whom do members try to develop contacts? Whom do they try to impress?	Interview; examine executive career lines to find units that provide avenues to the top.

Actors who hold power over one issue or area, such as influencing budget allocations, can lack power in another, such as determining long-term strategy. Although some studies report agreement among power measures (Brass & Burkhardt, 1993; Pfeffer, 1992), it is best to assess power using multiple measures and data-gathering techniques. If rankings vary by measure, investigators will need to obtain additional information to determine whether some of the measures are invalid or there are several distinct power bases in the organization.

Moreover, it is preferable to use issue-specific measures (Enz, 1989), along with general, global indicators.

Some authors have developed standard questionnaires for identifying powerful groups or individuals, delineating coalitions, describing prevalent influence tactics, and measuring power distribution. Many of these instruments use reputational techniques, in which respondents rank the power of other groups or individuals (Moch, Cammann, & Cooke, 1983; Nelson, 1988). Respondents usually have little difficulty in ranking the power or influence of their peers. Nonetheless, the data from studies such as these are often not valid enough to stand alone (Pfeffer, 1992).

As Table 4.2 indicates, a wide range of qualitative and largely unobtrusive techniques can supplement or substitute for questionnaire data on the power of political actors. Limitations in the measures can often be overcome through triangulation. Some of the strategies and methods listed in Table 4.2 can also provide data on the uses of power and its distribution. If practitioners observe the meetings of major decision-making forums, for example, they may obtain invaluable data on how members resolve differences and conflicts and the degree to which top executives share power with subordinates.

Unfortunately, many powerful forms of influence, particularly those that people regard as illegitimate, are difficult to observe. For example, coalition formation, agenda setting, manipulation, and informal deals can be hidden behind discourse that presents decisions as following organizationally rational procedures. Investigators who want to understand the actual, emergent practices of organizational politics will have to closely examine organizational documents, take note of interaction patterns among members of the focal organization, and listen carefully to what their informants tell them. To gather data on influence processes, consultants often rely on interviews, focus groups, or discussions during meetings or workshops. Consultants can ask members to provide detailed accounts of critical incidents, including organizational successes, the resolution of past organizational problems and crises, and the development of new ideas or proposals. In providing these accounts, members may, of course, justify and improve on their own behavior and that of others to whom they are loyal, and they may exaggerate the failings of those they hold in low esteem. Nonetheless, when interviews and group discussions are conducted and analyzed with sensitivity to these possibilities, they can provide insight into members' perceptions of political processes, key political actors, and influence tactics in use. To develop an understanding of power relations and processes that is independent of the perceptions of particular members, practitioners will have to carefully cross-check members' reports with one another and with other kinds of information.

EXERCISES

1. Assessing Fits

You may draw on your prior knowledge of an organization or gather basic organizational information and conduct several general orientation interviews (see Appendix A) before beginning this exercise. On a large sheet of newsprint or using a spreadsheet program, make a matrix listing as rows and columns all seven of the system components. Subdivide the Inputs (Resources) category into three categories: People (Human Resources), Knowledge and Information, and Material Resources. The matrix should be nine by nine. For each cell above the diagonal, ask how well the row entry (e.g., human resources) fits with the column entry (e.g., knowledge and informational resources). To make these queries more concrete, consider the questions about fit in Table 4.1. Where no question appears in the table, suggest your own. For example, do employees (human resources) have the knowledge needed to perform their tasks? If not, can they readily obtain it? Make notes on the degree of fit between each pair in your matrix. Be explicit about your criteria for assessing fit. After you have completed the matrix, note the two cases of poor fit that seem to produce the most serious instances of ineffectiveness or most severely constrain effectiveness. Be clear about your criteria for ineffectiveness or effectiveness. Write a report on these two cases in which you explain the nature of the lack of fit and its impact and make suggestions for improving the fits.

2. Emergent Practices: Rewards

Interview the head and at least one subordinate in a department or division. Use a list of guiding, open-ended questions about rewards and their relations to other features of the unit. In addition to writing your own questions, you may want to use questions from the General Orientation Interview in Appendix A. Cover the following issues in your interviews, and discuss each of them in your report:

- What are the main official types of rewards and sanctions, and what other rewards and sanctions are used in practice?

- What kinds of behavior are subject to rewards and sanctions? (Be specific.)

- What types of actions are encouraged and discouraged? (Consider hard work vs. taking it easy, personal loyalty to supervisors and peers, risk taking, exercising initiative, generating new ideas, and cooperation with others within or outside the unit.)

- Are the same rewards offered to everyone, or can people receive different types of rewards that are more appealing to them? (For example, one person may want a bonus, whereas another wants a chance to earn a degree while working.)

- How does each of the following influence the current system of rewards: peers, supervisor, higher-level management, and labor agreements?

If you have sufficient information, assess the fits between the current reward system and other system components (see Table 4.1).

3. Power to Act

Use at least two of the approaches listed in Table 4.2 to determine which people have the most power within some subunit of an organization, such as a branch, a division, or a department. Interview two of them about a major problem or challenge facing their unit. Find out during the interview or by another method whether they have the resources needed to deal with the problem. If not, specify what resources they would need to take action and what could be done to help them attain these resources or solve the problem some other way.

4. Stakeholder Analysis

Talk with a manager or organizational authority who can describe the individuals and groups within the organization and outside it who have a direct stake in a particular intervention—a step that management thinks might help solve a problem or enhance effectiveness. Identify other influential groups that would be indirectly affected by the decision. Ask the manager to describe how these stakeholders are likely to react to the intervention and how they reacted in the past to similar moves. Ask the manager to assess the power of each stakeholder and their capacity to act in support or opposition to the intervention. Organize your data in a chart with a row for each stakeholder. In the columns, summarize the stakeholders' interests, their position on the intervention, their power, the capacity for action, and the likely impact on the organization (ranked as strong, moderate, or weak). Write a summary describing your interview, the current balance of forces supporting and opposing the proposed intervention, and steps toward improvement that seem feasible in light of the forces shown in your table.

NOTES

1. See Harrison and Shirom (1999) for discussions of these types of consultant contributions to design change.
2. The original formulation of this approach by Ghoshal and Bartlett (1990) dealt with strategic business units (SBUs) in multinational firms. Corporate headquarters typically treat SBUs as semiautonomous investment centers.

3. The following discussion of lateral coordination draws on Galbraith (1977, 2002) and Galbraith et al. (1993).

4. On analysis of gaps between official and emergent behavior, see also Weisbord (1978) and Harrison and Shirom (1999, pp. 61–65, 235–243).

5. For further discussion of the diagnosis of power and politics, see Harrison and Shirom (1999, pp. 110–142) and Pfeffer (1992).

6. This section draws substantially on Pfeffer's (1981, pp. 35–65) discussion of assessing power. See also Finkelstein (1992) and Pfeffer (1992).

5

Environmental Relations

This chapter presents three analytic techniques for diagnosing organization-environment relations. Decision makers can also use these techniques as tools for planning ways to improve the focal organization's strategic position within its environment. Procedures for conducting in-depth interviews are discussed, along with other methods for gathering data on environmental relations.

Globalization, industrialization in China, recession and recovery, European unification, new digital technologies, financial reforms in health care, terrorism and antiterrorism, the paperless office, changing lifestyles, Mad Cow disease—the mass media provide a lengthy and rapidly changing list of developments that challenge today's organizations and sometimes create problems for them. Practitioners of diagnosis can make a major contribution to organizational performance by helping decision makers identify critical external conditions, assess current tactics for managing environmental relations, and find ways to improve these tactics and enhance their organization's competitive position. This chapter presents ways to conduct such diagnoses of environmental conditions and relations. Managers may also use this type of diagnosis to improve decision making and planning without the aid of consultants. The diagnostic models and techniques discussed here apply best to entire organizations or semiautonomous divisions but can also be adapted to less autonomous units. The lower the autonomy of a focal unit, the more its environment includes other units within the larger organization, including units at the same level in the hierarchy and top management.

GUIDELINES FOR DIAGNOSIS

Many analytical models and techniques have been developed to guide assessment of external relations.[1] Practitioners can use these techniques and frameworks to investigate a wide range of substantive issues. Consultants who adopt the sharp-image approach will focus on organization-environment relations that directly affect problems and challenges presented by clients. Consultants conducting a comprehensive diagnosis or supporting strategy formulation may scan a wide range of external conditions and organization-environment relations. The discussion that follows presents three techniques that illustrate the range of possible approaches and topical areas.

Environmental Relations Assessment

The environmental relations assessment (ERA) framework consists of the following six diagnostic guidelines that consultants and organizational members can apply to both for-profit and not-for-profit organizations:

1. *Identify key conditions in the task environment of the client organization (or unit).* Conditions that decisively influence the focal organization may include markets, sectoral and industry-wide conditions, technical and scientific conditions, labor pools, regulation, and competition. Key conditions for a firm providing wind power and other environmentally friendly sources of energy, for example, include markets for its products, competition, underlying technologies, governmental regulations affecting the prices and delivery of cleaner forms of energy, availability and cost of generation and transmission facilities, and talent pools from which the firm recruits its personnel. External stakeholders who are affected by the firm's actions and try to influence its operations may include environmental and political groups that favor or oppose the use of particular sites for generation (e.g., banks of wind turbines) and transmission (e.g., power lines), along with national agencies and public interest groups concerned with nonenvironmental issues, such as minority employment and employee health. Public agencies and service organizations are especially subject to pressures and constraints from external regulatory and certifying bodies.

2. *Specify the main organizations with which the client organization interacts, characterize its relations with them, and specify the demands or constraints created by the most powerful external organizations.* Outside organizations may include suppliers, consumers of goods and services, supervisory and regulatory groups, unions, competitors, community and political stakeholders, and non-managing owners (e.g., stockholders). Structural relations with these organizations can range from competition to cooperation. They can also include hierarchical links, such as supervision and ownership. The most powerful external organizations should be listed, along with the main demands or organizational constraints generated by them. To assess the power of external organizations, practitioners can examine the focal organization's dependence on them for vital resources and the dependence of these organizations on the client organization. Resource dependence gives the supplier of the needed resource

power over the recipient (Pfeffer & Salancik, 2003). It is also important to consider the munificence of resource flows from the environment.

3. *Note the main units and individuals who handle external contacts.* In addition to noting formal responsibilities for functions such as strategy formation, sales, public relations, fund-raising, and staff recruitment, practitioners can examine which people or groups fill these roles in practice. Techniques such as responsibility charting (see Chapter 4) may prove useful if there is confusion or disagreement about who handles critical external relations.

4. *Examine current responses to external problems and demands.* Organizations can respond to external pressures by avoiding them, making internal adjustments, or intervening in the environment to reduce pressures or shape demands at their source (Pfeffer & Salancik, 2003). Within these broad categories, there are a range of possible options. Avoidance techniques include simply ignoring external demands; delaying actions; and responding to pressures through largely symbolic actions, such as renaming existing activities to fit new expectations or creating a committee that is assigned responsibility for an issue but receives little power to change things. Options for internal adjustment include acceding to demands in ways that create minimum disruptions of organizational routines; making temporary or periodic changes in staffing, work rates, or activities to cope with shifts in demand or resources; monitoring external developments to reduce surprises and facilitate planning; and redesigning structures and processes to align them with environmental contingencies (see Chapter 4). For example, the heads of a junior college could respond symbolically to increasing student demand for computer training by announcing far-off and tentative plans to revamp their curriculum. More action-oriented responses would include adding advanced courses in computer skills or mandating inclusion of computer training in existing courses.

In contrast to such forms of internal adaptation, organizations intervene in their environments through political actions (e.g., lobbying), use of economic power (e.g., demanding low prices from suppliers that depend on them for business), advertising to shape demand and attitudes, creating short-term or lasting alliances with other organizations, and changing their mix of products and services so as to enter new environmental niches.

Choice among responses will reflect an organization's past practices, organizational politics, and prevailing beliefs in addition to reasoned considerations of the costs and benefits of alternative lines of action. The effects of beliefs and norms are well illustrated by organizational responses to signs of a downturn in performance (Ford & Baucus, 1987). Decision makers may favor ignoring these signs and riding out the downturn, making incremental adjustments, or taking strategic action to change internal or external conditions. The choice among these options and the particular steps chosen will reflect the decision makers' judgments concerning the likely length of the downturn, its severity, its causes, and their organization's capability to ride it out or to take strategic action to reverse the trend.

5. *Assess the effectiveness of current responses to the environment.* Ideally, consultants and their clients will evaluate recent internal adjustments and environmental interventions in terms of agreed-upon effectiveness criteria. In the case of the junior college, no extra funds were available for computer training, so its costs had to be balanced by increased revenues. Therefore, in terms of budgetary considerations, adding courses that could attract additional students, as well as serve current students, would be a more effective response than introducing computer training into existing courses. Course enrollment fees could generate additional revenues, whereas the purchase and support of computer equipment and software for use in existing courses would add expenses without generating revenues.

The system resource and adaptation criteria listed in Table 2.1 can serve as standards for evaluating the impacts of organizational efforts to manage external relations. These criteria emphasize the quality and quantity of resources obtained and the ability of the organization to adapt to external change. Particularly important are indicators of the organization's strategic position, including changes in revenues, market share, and external ratings and reputation. In addition, effectiveness can be defined in terms of the organization's ability to create favorable external conditions in which to operate.

Practitioners can also evaluate tactics for managing environmental relations in terms of their effects on internal processes. For example, if an organization uses tactics that limit external interference in the work flow, then work routines can more readily be established and less expensive and complex forms of coordination can be used. If external forces create chronic problems and crises, or disruptions periodically reach major proportions, then current responses may be judged to be inadequate. Other signs of ineffective tactics include severe internal tensions and conflicts that result from external pressures or reliance on stopgap techniques that delay serious management of external threats until they reach crisis proportions.

6. *Search for ways to improve management of environmental relations.* Before recommending far-reaching changes, consultants and clients should first consider ways to improve current practices or make incremental changes that help manage external relations. For instance, a national park that suffers from increasing overcrowding during peak season can expand the number of campgrounds requiring reservations, or it might begin restricting day access to overcrowded areas.

If effectiveness cannot be achieved by incremental changes, strategic changes might be considered. Organizations may redesign the way they conduct core processes, and they may enter new fields of business or markets by changing their mix of products and service or changing the basis of competition (e.g., service vs. price). For example, a municipal hospital serving publicly insured patients might offer laboratory or diagnostic services at private-sector rates to patients who would not otherwise use the hospital's services.

To develop practical recommendations for improving external relations, practitioners need to listen carefully to suggestions by members of the organization who will be responsible for implementing these steps. It is important to pay close attention to these actors' concerns about possible barriers to implementing change. Strategic changes, in particular, are difficult to accomplish, require substantial investments of time and money, and often produce unanticipated and undesirable effects on system components and subcomponents that were not direct targets for change. Hence, consultants and managers need to pay attention to the organization's readiness and capacity for change and carefully weigh expected benefits of reorganizations against their potential costs and negative consequences.

Among the advantages of ERA analysis are its broad applicability and its inclusion of an explicit assessment of the outcomes of current ways of handling external demands. In addition, ERA allows consultants to focus on specific external demands or developments that create operating difficulties for the client organization. Disadvantages of the technique include its lack of explicit focus on the competitive environment in which firms and many not-for-profits operate and its concentration on current conditions.[2] Moreover, ERA's complexity makes it time-consuming and poses barriers to involving members of the client organization in the diagnostic process. The two techniques discussed in the following sections address one or more of these disadvantages.

Competitive Strategy Analysis Through SWOT

The search for competitive advantage forms the heart of many strategy formulation techniques.[3] These techniques attribute an organization's strategic advantage to distinctive competencies that help it deliver a product or service that is superior in price, quality, or terms of delivery to products offered by competitors. Many public-sector organizations and some private ones enjoy an advantageous environmental position because they are sole or dominant suppliers of a product or service. Nonetheless, an increasing number of public organizations are competing for funds, clientele, and public support with other

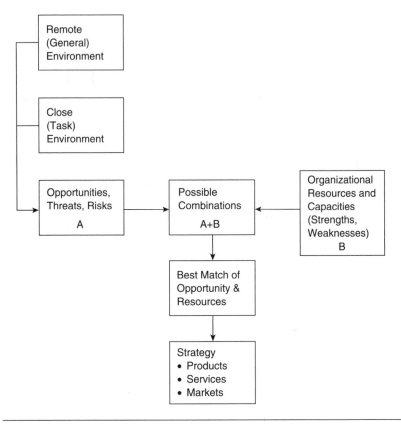

Figure 5.1   Model for Strategy Formulation

public agencies or with privately owned organizations. As a result, competitive strategy analysis has become increasingly relevant to organizations in the public sector as well as to firms and not-for-profit organizations.

The popular SWOT technique seeks the best match between organizational capacities (strengths and weaknesses) and environmental conditions (opportunities and threats). Figure 5.1 provides a schematic summary of strategy formulation based on SWOT, as envisioned by Andrews (1980) and others.

Threats are defined as threats to competitive position. Opportunities are situations that organizations might exploit to improve their competitive advantage or overcome threats. Potentially important sources of threats and opportunities in the general environment include political, economic, social, and technological developments at local, regional, national, and international levels. These forces can shape many crucial conditions in the task environment, including demand for products or services; support and legitimating of organizational actions; flows of human and material resources; and costs, work processes, and other operating conditions. Behavioral science consultants can sometimes make an important contribution to the analysis of external developments by pointing to potential impacts of difficult to measure, but nonetheless influential, developments in fields such as social issues, culture, and politics.

Features of the firm's task environment shape competition for customers, clients, and resources. Technical analytical tools (Porter, 1998a, 1998b) are typically used to analyze the competitive environment of firms. The system model presented in Chapter 2 and other popular diagnostic models (Harrison & Shirom, 1999, chap. 4) can guide the analysis of other features of the firm's task environment. These models can also structure an analysis of the task environment of not-for-profit organizations.

Organizational strengths are capacities that enhance competitive advantage or provide the potential to do so. Organizational weaknesses are functional problems or limits on capabilities. These weaknesses, along with resource constraints, can undermine an organization's competitive position or prevent it from taking advantage of market opportunities.

By comparing organizational strengths to environmental opportunities, decision makers can identify an organization's distinctive competencies. Examination of the resources available for supporting a strategy further contributes to analysis of strategic capabilities. It is important to scan financial, managerial, technical, knowledge, and political capabilities along with competencies in functional areas, such as human resource management and marketing. Functional areas in which industrial firms can develop distinctive competencies include technology and the development, design, production, and distribution of products (Porter, 1998b). In particular, consultants and their clients need to look beyond current activities as they identify underlying organizational capabilities, including capacities for innovation and learning, that can be translated into new products and services. Similarly, the assessment should consider prospects for increasing organizational capabilities and overcoming weaknesses. For example, possible strategic contributions of training and other human resource management functions can be examined.

After assessing internal and external conditions, managers and consultants can seek the best match between external opportunities and organizational resources and capacities. Identification of this match leads to choices about business strategy and in particular to decisions concerning the desired mix of products, services, and markets; ways to compete on costs; and ways to differentiate products on attributes, such as quality and accessibility (Porter, 1998a).

SWOT analysis contributes to development of strategy by helping decision makers and their consultants search for additional profitable products or services that the organization can provide at lower cost or higher quality than can competitors. Suppose, for example, that an architectural firm currently concentrates on designing factories and warehouses for commercial enterprises. Although the firm is highly expert in this type of design and receives most of its current revenue from this type of service, competition in this niche is very stiff and becoming even stronger. In contrast, the firm may possess a distinctive competence in the design of retirement facilities—an activity that currently provides only a small fraction of the firm's revenue but offers many opportunities for growth. Recognition of this distinctive competence can lead to a redirection of activities into this previously neglected market niche.

As noted in Chapter 2, the SWOT framework can be expanded to support broader, system-oriented diagnoses of organization-environment relations. For this purpose, threats are defined to include any condition that produces or is expected to harm effectiveness by generating declines in critical system inputs, throughputs, or outputs. Opportunities include any kind of opportunity to overcome threats, enhance resource flows, or otherwise improve effectiveness. In addition to features directly enhancing strategic position, organizational strengths are defined as including all success factors that enhance effectiveness or provide the potential to do so. In like manner, weaknesses include all internal forces that undermine effectiveness, along with forces blocking plans to enhance operations.

When SWOT analyses aim to enhance business strategies, they are usually conducted by experts in fields such as marketing, industry analysis, and business strategy. Change management consultants could readily lead more system-oriented SWOT analyses. The results of either type of SWOT analysis can serve as inputs to strategy formulation by clients. SWOT can also be used by members of an organization in self-diagnosis or in a consultant-facilitated process that remains client centered. The simplicity of the SWOT concepts makes them appropriate to such participative processes. Participants in SWOT studies, however, may lack the expertise needed to assess external developments. Moreover, they may legitimately disagree on the nature of external conditions and their implications for the organization. Thus, client-centered SWOT sessions may not result in much agreement or certainty as to whether particular developments pose threats or create opportunities, how their effects will be felt, and how the organization might best respond to them. Consultants and clients interested in strategy development should also bear in mind the limitations of systematic strategic planning techniques (Mintzberg, 1994); in many successful firms, strategy formation is less deliberate, less planful, and much more emergent than the highly analytic process embodied in techniques such as SWOT and open systems planning.

Open Systems Planning

Open systems planning (OSP) is a client-centered diagnostic intervention. Participants in OSP are members of an organization or subunit who have responsibility and authority to engage in strategic decision making and planning. The consultant facilitates and guides the discussions, records and summarizes them, and gives feedback without dictating the content of the diagnosis and the planning. Groups whose members are familiar with OSP's background and approach can also use it without the aid of an external consultant. The following summary of the main steps in OSP includes instructions to participants in the planning process:[4]

1. *Analyze current environmental conditions.* Create a map of the external conditions, groups, and organizations in the task environment and the demands, problems, and opportunities created by these forces.

2. *Analyze current responses to the environment.* Describe the ways that the organization handles these environmental demands and conditions. Consider all important transactions with the task environment.

3. *Analyze actual priorities and purposes.* Define current goals, values, and priorities by examining current responses to the environment and the organization's internal features (structure, processes, culture, etc.). If possible, reach agreement on the organization's guiding mission.

4. *Predict trends and conditions.* Predict likely changes in external conditions during the next 2–5 years. Assess the future of the organization if it maintains its current responses to the environment.

5. *Define an ideal future.* Create scenarios for an ideal future state that can envision changes in the organizational purposes and priorities, external conditions, and responses to the environment.

6. *Compare current and ideal states.* In light of projected trends (step 4), define gaps between current and ideal future states in purposes, external conditions, and organizational responses. These gaps may be thought of as differences between where the organization seems to be going and where you want it to go.

7. *Establish priorities.* Assign priorities to the gaps between ideal and current conditions. Define areas of working agreement and identify disagreements about values, priorities, and purposes.

8. *Plan appropriate action.* Plan ways of moving toward agreed upon future states by narrowing the most important gaps identified in stages 6 and 7. Plan immediate actions and those to be undertaken after 6 months and 2 years. Consider actions for resolving disagreements. Create a schedule for following up on actions and updating plans.

Like other client-centered diagnostic interventions, OSP may enhance decision making and learning capacity in client organizations. Moreover, like other popular collaborative approaches (Jimenez, Escalante, & Aguirre-Vazquez, 1997; Weisbord, 1988), OSP encourages envisioning possible organizational futures and adoption of a proactive stance toward the environment. Nonetheless, OSP shares many of the potential disadvantages of client-centered diagnosis (see Chapter 1) and should be used only in situations in which participants possess the team skills and constructive problem-solving approach required by this type of collaborative analysis and decision making.

DIAGNOSTIC METHODS

Data Gathering

Direct Investigation

If possible, practitioners should gather data from members of the focal organization's environment in much the same ways that they obtain information from inside the focal organization. Direct investigations of the environment can help members of the client organization look at their strengths and weaknesses through the eyes of powerful groups in their environment (Morgan, 1988). Consultants may interview key clients, customers, and even competitors and representatives of stakeholder groups. For example, a diagnostic practitioner might interview the head of an environmental defense group that opposes expansion of the client's physical plant. Outside experts can also be consulted on topics such as the state of the industry or sector in which the client organization operates.

As Case 8 suggests, interviews with people outside an organization can sometimes shed light on critical organization-environment relations and stimulate efforts to improve these relations.

Case 8

As part of an organizational diagnosis focused on quality improvement, the human resources specialist in a high-technology firm asked key customers to assess the firm's performance. Interviews with customers covered their involvement in the development of new products and assessed support and service after delivery. Feedback from these interviews to line managers within the firm helped them understand the importance of quality management and served as a stimulus for improvements in product development, support, and service.

Valuable information about external conditions and relations can also be obtained from the daily press and business publications, information sources such as Standard & Poor's (Kinnear & Taylor, 1995), and organizational documents (Stewart, 1992). Much information is available on the World Wide Web. In addition to information on business environments, documentation may be available on sectors such as health, social services, and education, in which many public organizations and not-for-profit organizations operate. Practitioners need to pay close attention to the sources of information, whether it is online or in print; it is important to bear in mind the purposes for which information is disseminated (e.g., public relations, marketing, research, and evaluation by a governmental body). Practitioners can also consult outside experts on topics such as the state of an industry or technology. Additional data may derive from market research and business planning studies conducted for the client organization before the diagnosis or in parallel with it.

Indirect Investigation

Unfortunately, practical constraints and considerations of client discretion often prevent direct access to people outside of the client organization. In such cases, practitioners gather information about environmental relations primarily through interviews with top management and other officials with responsibility for handling specific types of external relations (e.g., sales, public relations, customer service, and fundraising). These interviews can include questions such as those in Appendix A, Sections IV, V, and X, which shed light on organization-environment fits.

Constructing an Interview Guide

Rather than preparing specific questions in advance, investigators with experience in semistructured interviewing may prefer to gather data on environmental relations, as well as on other system features, through interviews based on an interview guide. The guide lists topics to be investigated and allows the interviewer to frame questions about each topic that reflect the distinctive circumstances of the client organization; the guide also provides opportunities to take into account previous answers. Interview guides thus ensure coverage of major topics while allowing flexibility. Interview guides have lower reliability than standardized questionnaires, however, because they allow for more variation between interviews and among interviewers. Using interview guides also requires more interviewer skill than does the use of more structured schedules.

Here is an illustration of the major headings for an interview guide based on the ERA:

1. Key external conditions in markets or fields
2. Main outside organizations, types of relations (ties, competition vs. cooperation, resource dependence)
3. Main units, people who handle external contacts
4. Current management of problems, demands, opportunities
5. Effectiveness of current actions, including specification of effectiveness criteria
6. Ways to improve current environmental management

Each major heading in the guide would be broken down into subheadings to cover specific topics. For example, Items 4 and 5 could be specified as follows:

4.   Current management of problems, demands, opportunities

4.1. Specific actions—describe in detail. What is/was done, by whom? (Search for internal adjustments, interventions in environment; incremental vs. strategic actions.)

4.2. Other actions (e.g., Did your group make any other attempts to moderate these pressures/deflect these criticisms/anticipate such developments, etc.?) (Interviewer, Note anticipatory vs. reactive moves.)

5.   Effectiveness of current actions

5.1. External impact of actions

5.1.1. Impacts on external actors, conditions (e.g., How did x react to the steps you took?)

5.1.2. Effectiveness (Use effectiveness criteria suggested by respondent; e.g., Did these steps improve your sales revenues?)

5.2. Internal organizational impacts (Probe for felt effects of one-time or recurring reliance on these responses, whether they produced desired results, how successful they seemed to respondent, and meaning of success for him or her.)

5.3. Changes in tactics and impacts. Were similar problems handled in the same way in the past? What happened after changes in tactics? (Probe for shifts in tactics, stance toward environment, and variations in impacts.)

When practitioners use an interview guide, they prepare for the possibility that the answers will range across the topics listed in the guide. During the interview, they record the responses in the order given. Afterward, they can reorganize them according to the topics in the guide.

Questionnaires

Some standardized questionnaires include reliable, structured measures of external relations and conditions. These measures can facilitate comparisons between units within a large organization or among organizations. For example, the Organizational Assessment Inventory (Van de Ven & Ferry, 1980; Appendix B in this volume) contains measures of perceived environmental predictability (Van de Ven & Ferry, 1980, pp. 241–258) and dependence on external organizations (Gresov, 1989). Many of the items included in the Organizational Assessment Inventory apply to both for-profit and not-for-profit organizations. The International Organizational Observatory (Heijltjes, 2000; Heijltjes & van Witteloostuijn, 1996), an instrument developed for comparisons among European businesses, includes measures of interorganizational linkages (e.g., joint ventures, licensing, and franchising), market conditions, anticipated external developments and responses, overall competitive position, and competitive position on major products. The National Organizations Survey (Kalleberg, Marsden, Spaeth, & Knoke, 1996; Appendix B in this volume) includes measures of how employers interact with other organizations to obtain and train new workers. Although useful, measures such as these will not provide the wealth of data obtainable through interviews or questionnaires that are tailored to the client organization.

Analysis and Feedback

Data Analysis and Interpretation

Models that specify links between environmental conditions, strategies, and organizational design features can help practitioners examine fits between external conditions and features of the client organization. For example, practitioners can assess whether coordination mechanisms are appropriate to environmental conditions that are very dynamic and difficult to interpret. Units that face very unpredictable environments (e.g., threats of bioterrorism) or poorly understood tasks (e.g., resolving community conflict) will usually need to make more use of complex, lateral coordination mechanisms and organic administrative systems than will units dealing with predictable environments.

Another analytical approach involves examining the uses and consequences of each of the response tactics listed in ERA guideline No. 4. In this way, consultants can uncover ways to make current tactics more effective and discover neglected possibilities for managing external relations. An additional procedure for mapping external contacts is described in Exercise 1.

Except in very small organizations, each unit in a client organization will deal with a different subenvironment consisting of those sectors of the environment most relevant to the unit's operations. To analyze environmental relations in complex organizations, practitioners need to construct profiles of the main features of the subenvironments of major units. These profiles can note features such as the following:

- Predictability (ability to anticipate external developments)
- Complexity (number of relevant external organizations and degree of difference between them)
- Competitiveness
- Dependence on other organizations
- Degree of economic and political threat or support to the unit and the organization as a whole
- Distinctive problems and challenges
- Tactics for managing external relations

To make characterizations of the environments faced by an entire organization or division, practitioners will often have to create a composite picture drawn from the reports of people who are knowledgeable about particular subenvironments. Similarly, practitioners can synthesize data from subunits to assess organization-wide impacts of tactics for managing external relations. To decide which responses to the environment work best, practitioners can compare past responses to current ones or contrast the approaches of units or organizations facing similar conditions.

Preparations for Feedback

Feedback of data on environmental relations can focus directly on the effectiveness of current tactics for managing these relations and ways to enhance effectiveness. Alternatively, practitioners can present the findings on the state of the environment and external relations as stimuli for self-analysis and decision making. In preparing the data for analysis and feedback, consultants should examine how the members of the client organization are reading external conditions and interpreting important environmental developments (Weitzel & Jonsson, 1991). Interpretations of the environment are shaped by many factors, including the members' position in the organization, their work experience and training, their social and cultural backgrounds, their personalities, and the organizational culture. Sometimes members of an organization systematically deny or ignore developments such as client dissatisfaction or sectoral trends, which the consultant and outsiders, such as industry experts, regard as critical. Judicious feedback about gaps between internal and external views of the organization can help members become aware of how others view them and can motivate them to take action to improve external relations.

EXERCISES

1. External Contacts

Choose a unit within an organization that has substantial external contacts (both within and outside the organization's boundaries). Interview the head of the unit using Sections IV and V of the General Orientation Interview (Appendix A). Make a chart showing the focal unit at the center and the other units and groups around it. Then color code the chart to show the external groups or units on which the focal unit is most dependent for resources or services, ones with which contact is most frequent, and any outside units or organizations that have authority over the focal unit. Describe the routines and procedures linking the focal unit to two of the most important external units. Indicate how these procedures could be improved, and suggest other ways for improving relations with these important units.

2. Environmental Relations Assessment

Construct a detailed interview guide that reflects the issues treated in the six guidelines for ERA. Using this guide, interview the head of a unit or small organization. Organize the responses to the interview and your conclusions about it in terms of the categories given in the guidelines.

3. SWOT

Construct an interview guide based on the SWOT model and Figure 5.1. Interview at least two top managers in a firm or a not-for-profit organization that competes for clients or critical resources. Include questions on the firm's general and task environments, all four SWOT components, and current and possible future strategies for attaining competitive advantage. Write a report evaluating current strategies and (if appropriate) recommending strategy changes. Be sure to explain how the proposed changes are likely to enhance competitive advantage.

NOTES

1. See Bunker and Alban (2002), Cummings and Worley (2001), and Harrison and Shirom (1999, chaps. 2, 11–14) for additional models and techniques.

2. Future-oriented guidelines can be added to ERA. For example, "Identify external trends that are creating new problems or opportunities or are likely to do so in the future," and "Consider possible responses to anticipated developments." See also the discussions of SWOT and OSP.

3. These techniques assume that strategy is deliberately and systematically formulated by top managers. See Mintzberg, Lampel, Quinn, and Ghoshal (2003) and Harrison and Shirom (1999, pp. 349–373) on nondeliberate processes of strategy formation.

4. This summary, which synthesizes and slightly adapts Jayaram's (1976) approach, also draws on Burke (1982, p. 66) and Plovnick, Fry, and Burke (1982, pp. 69–70). The main advantages of Jayaram's approach over that of Beckhard and Harris (1977, pp. 58–69) are that it allows the definitions of purposes and priorities to emerge from the discussions of the current and ideal states and requires only the achievement of working agreements about operating priorities. This approach to defining goals and priorities seems more realistic than expecting participants to agree in advance on the organization's core mission (Fry, 1982).

6

Challenges and Dilemmas of Diagnosis

Successful diagnosis requires practitioners to meet the requirements of diagnostic process, modeling, and methods and achieve a good balance between handling diagnostic tasks in all three areas. In addition, practitioners must make difficult choices concerning project goals, the groups and individuals who are to benefit from diagnosis, and professional standards and personal values and interests. In this chapter, these choices are presented in terms of three diagnostic dilemmas. Practitioners may enhance their chances of conducting useful and influential diagnoses by confronting these dilemmas and working with their clients to resolve them in practical and mutually acceptable ways.

The preceding chapters presented organizational diagnosis as an effort to help client organizations solve problems and chart routes toward enhancing organizational effectiveness.[1] To accomplish these objectives, consultants must deal with three diverse challenges and achieve a good balance among their tactics for handling each challenge. The processual challenge requires constructive management of interactions with clients and other organizational stakeholders. The methodological challenge calls for using rigorous and valid techniques for gathering, summarizing, and analyzing data within the constraints imposed by the consulting assignment. The analytic challenge involves using research-based models to identify sources of effectiveness and ineffectiveness, discover routes toward organizational improvement, and frame feedback.

Despite their usefulness, the models discussed in this book and other models like them cannot serve as step-by-step guides to diagnosis. Nor can they be used like equations into which bits of data are inserted to produce a completed assessment. No such recipes for diagnosis or action planning exist, and none is likely to be discovered. Instead, most models work best as frames and guides that help both experienced and beginning practitioners sort out what is going on within an organization. Because models focus attention on particular system levels or types of phenomena, they may distract attention from other important organizational features. Only by combining these partial frames can practitioners deal with the multifaceted nature of organizational problems and challenges (Harrison & Shirom, 1999).

Anyone who undertakes a diagnosis thus faces many choices about which models and methods to use and how to manage the consulting process. In most cases, each alternative has some advantages and some drawbacks. Emerging relations between clients and practitioners and practical considerations, such as the accessibility of data, shape choices among alternatives. Beginning practitioners will need firsthand experience in diagnosis and consulting processes and further training in organizational analysis and research methods to develop the ability to make these judgments.

This chapter locates the immediate choices facing practitioners within the broader context of three types of dilemmas:

- *Goals dilemma*—pursuing modest objectives that can be obtained quickly and easily versus pursuing more promising and ambitious objectives that require more effort and are riskier
- *Politics dilemma*—seeking benefits for all members of a client organization versus providing selective benefits
- *Professionalism dilemma*—maintaining strict professional standards versus responding to personal needs and interests

These dilemmas capture central issues facing practitioners and their clients as they negotiate the nature of a diagnostic project. Although the dilemmas confront consultants whose interventions in the client organization go beyond diagnosis, this chapter concentrates on the implications for diagnostic work.

By considering these dilemmas before beginning a project, practitioners may be better equipped to handle their emerging relations with clients. As they negotiate with clients, practitioners will need to find ways to raise and clarify the issues highlighted by the diagnostic dilemmas to ensure mutually compatible expectations for the diagnosis. These dilemmas can only be resolved provisionally and partially. Hence, consultants will need to reconsider them as the diagnostic project unfolds and changes occur in their own needs and expectations and those of their clients.

THE GOALS DILEMMA

Hierarchy of Goals

Possible goals for diagnosis can be ranked in the following hierarchy, which starts with more focused and less ambitious goals:[2]

1. Provide specific information or evaluation. For example, assess the effects of a new customer relations program or evaluate whether day care programs enable mothers to take full-time jobs.

2. Solve a specific problem or reduce ineffectiveness. For example, improve public satisfaction with an organization's services or reduce work accidents and errors.

3. Assess organizational effectiveness and recommend ways to improve effectiveness.

4. Contribute to organizational learning by helping members of the client organization enhance their capacities to handle problems and challenges and build these enhanced capacities into organizational processes, structures, and culture.

5. Contribute to organizational transformation by helping top management make fundamental changes in key system features, including goals and strategies, structures, processes, technology, and culture.

The first two goals focus on short-term, incremental improvements, whereas the fourth and fifth goals envision long-term, fundamental impacts. Depending on the effectiveness criteria used, the third goal may aim at either incremental or fundamental, strategic improvements. Practitioners can usually achieve the first objective through a straightforward assessment or evaluation study, without diagnosing forces that lie behind the issue being examined. The second goal requires diagnostic modeling but defines the diagnostic task in a highly focused manner. In some cases, problem-solving studies can be quite routine. However, when ineffectiveness is chronic and the sources of ineffective behavior run broad and deep within the organization (e.g., errors in hospitals), reducing ineffectiveness will be quite challenging. Achieving the more ambitious, higher-level goals requires even greater investments of time and effort by both clients and consultants and is riskier.

Sources of Tension and Conflict

There are at least three sources of the goals dilemma: (a) potential incompatibilities among goals, (b) divergences in goal preferences within the client organization or between clients and consultants, and (c) tensions between incentives and disincentives to pursue higher-level goals.

Conflicting Goals

Conflicts or tensions between goals arise because the successful achievement of a goal at any given level in the goals hierarchy may block pursuit of a goal at a different level. For instance, practitioners who accept their clients' definitions of the information needs or problems facing an organization and agree to pursue a very narrow and modest diagnostic goal may find themselves focusing their attention on symptoms of ineffectiveness while neglecting their underlying causes. High staff turnover, for example, may reflect a wide range of underlying problems—including poor interpersonal relations, limited opportunities for individual initiative and innovation, and internal conflict—as well as more obvious weaknesses in reward systems or opportunities for advancement.

Similarly, systematically pursuing the goal of improving effectiveness may actually block the consultant's ability to contribute to organizational learning. Consider the consultant who recommends sophisticated changes in organizational design to take advantage of innovations in information technology. Although these changes may enhance current effectiveness, they will not necessarily empower members of the organization to design and implement the next generation of needed design innovations on their own. On the contrary, the sophistication of the consultant's recommendations may deepen the clients' dependence on outside expertise. In other words, successful pursuit of a lower-level goal may undercut the achievement of a higher-level one. Moreover, by pursuing higher-level goals, practitioners may neglect their clients' more immediate objectives and thereby fail to meet their expectations.

An additional source of incompatibility among these goals lies in the tendency for clients and other influential members of the focal organization to type consultants in terms of particular project objectives and intervention styles. Suppose, for example, that a consultant's first project with a client group involves gathering data on the attitudes of managers toward relocating geographically and recommending appropriate incentives for relocation. After the project becomes known within the organization, its members may associate the consultant with that type of detailed fact finding and problem solving and may, therefore, assume that the consultant is not capable of conducting broader projects that have higher-level objectives.

Disagreement About Goals

The second source of the goals dilemma stems from gaps between consultants' goal preferences and those of their clients and from gaps among goals held by various members of the client organization. Clients often prefer lower-level goals because they promise concrete results with limited costs. In contrast, consultants often aim for higher-level goals because projects directed to these goals are longer, more labor-intensive, and more lucrative. In addition, pursuit of higher-level goals offers consultants the possibility of making a major contribution to a client organization and is often more professionally challenging than handling routine assignments. Hence, consultants may feel torn between pressing for pursuit of higher-level goals and satisfying the expectations of clients who want immediate, certain results.

Disagreement about project goals among powerful stakeholders within and outside the client organization may also occur because the potential risks and benefits of pursuing any particular project goal are not shared equally. For instance, the management of a large division might call on internal consultants to assess the overall operations of one of their units. In contrast, to reduce the threat of negative findings, the heads of that unit may press for a narrower definition of the study's goals.

Costs Versus Benefits

The goals dilemma also stems from tension between the substantial benefits that both clients and consultants may gain from pursuing higher-level goals and the costs and risks of pursuing these goals. Understandably, clients often express concerns about the costs of entering into expensive, time-consuming projects that may yield few results. Clients may also resist studies aimed at improving overall effectiveness or enhancing learning because these ambitious projects require greater client commitment than narrowly focused investigations and are more likely to reveal weaknesses within top management.

Despite the professional and financial appeals of ambitious projects, consultants also face deterrents to pursuing higher-level diagnostic goals. Pursuit of higher-level goals requires consultants to be more skilled in managing the consulting process. Moreover, projects with higher-level goals expose consultants to greater risks of client dissatisfaction and project failure than does the pursuit of lower-level goals. Many structural, interpersonal, and psychological forces may prevent members of an organization from unlearning ingrained habits and approaches and replacing these habits with alternative ways of thinking and acting. In fact, fundamental changes in organizational culture are not often achieved, unless the organization goes through a major crisis and new leadership emerges or is imposed from above.

Partial Resolutions

Although there is no simple solution to the goals dilemma, several partial resolutions are possible. One popular approach is to begin a project by pursuing lower-level diagnostic goals and define higher-level goals only after early successes. This technique of sequencing goals can help consultants and clients pursue what would otherwise be incompatible goals, provided that consultants can avoid being typed as capable of handling only lower-level objectives. Changing gradually from lower- to higher-level goals can also build trust between consultants and clients, enhance consultants' knowledge of the organization before ambitious projects are planned and build the motivation and skills that clients need to pursue difficult projects.

Divergences between goal preferences within the client organization can also be provisionally resolved. When consultants discover such divergences, they can provide feedback on these goal conflicts to clients and request that they reach a working agreement on the study's objectives and priorities before the diagnosis proceeds further. Sequencing diagnostic projects can also help reduce goal divergences within the organization or between clients and consultants, because members of the client organization can usually reach agreement more readily concerning the pursuit of more modest objectives. For this reason, it is often easier and more fruitful to focus diagnoses on reducing ineffectiveness, rather than on enhancing effectiveness. The multiple stakeholder approach (see Chapter 2) suggests another possibility: conducting the diagnosis to report on the major lines of disagreement among organizational stakeholders and assessing how the organization handles these differences.

THE POLITICS DILEMMA

Who Benefits[3]

Who is to benefit from the diagnostic study—the client who originally sponsored the study, a particular organizational stratum such as top management, all members of a unit or group whose problem was originally presented to the consultant, or the entire organization? This question captures the essence of the politics dilemma: No matter how cooperative and consensual relations are within an organization, some groups and individuals will benefit more than others from a diagnostic study, and some may be harmed by it.

The most obvious reason that diagnosis may threaten or harm people is that it may uncover performance weaknesses or organizational failings for which the people will be accountable. In addition, diagnostic recommendations may suggest enhancing the resources or authority of particular individuals or units. Diagnosis can also have a differential impact on particular members or units, because the process of providing people with additional information and understanding about their organization's operations may increase their power or their ability to take particular actions. There may also be hidden power implications in the ways in which clients and practitioners define problems and selectively focus on some organizational levels or features—for example, labor costs among lower-level employees, as opposed to managerial practices and organization designs that generate hidden costs and reduce productivity.

Diagnostic recommendations may also support particular value positions at the expense of others. If, for example, consultants recommend that managers delegate more authority and increase participation in decision making, these recommendations may clash with the values and interests of managers who benefit personally from the current concentration of power. It should be no surprise, then, that people who sense that they stand to gain from a diagnosis will applaud and support the decision to conduct the study, whereas those who expect to lose may oppose it or cooperate only reluctantly. Consultants must therefore decide who are to be the main beneficiaries of their work and what their stance will be toward members who may be threatened by the diagnosis.

Some Solutions

A wide variety of partial resolutions of the politics dilemma are possible. These range from the pole of seeking to provide benefits to all members of an organization to that of treating the diagnosis as a service to the specific clients who called for the study. According to the former view, which dominated much of the early organization development literature, consultants are obligated to strive to improve the organization as a whole, not to enhance the position of individuals within it. The goals of diagnosis and intervention are therefore defined as the ultimate improvement of organizational properties, such as health, effectiveness, or cohesion. This attempt to benefit all members of the client organization may be criticized for overlooking the realities of power and politics. By focusing on abstract organizational states, consultants may overlook the concrete relations among the people who are affected by the diagnosis. Moreover, practitioners who focus mainly on abstract organizational states may give themselves so much freedom to define what is good for the organization that they end up pursuing project goals or making recommendations that are not widely understood or accepted within the organization.

Although there are limitations to focusing on overall organizational states, this approach does give added significance to two ethical mandates that apply to practitioners of diagnosis as well as other consultants, no matter how they solve the politics dilemma. First, consultants must preserve the confidentiality of information obtained about individual members of the organization. Second, consultants should seek to avoid unjustifiable harm to the interests of individual members of the client organization. When consultants seek to produce benefits for the entire organization, these two responsibilities become practical necessities and ethical obligations. If diagnosis is justified by its contribution to the organization as a whole, consultants avoid diagnosing the performance of specific individuals within the organization; instead, practitioners concentrate on the performance of entire organizational units and on systemic sources of problems. From this perspective, practitioners should not make recommendations concerning the hiring, placement, or retention of individuals, nor should they report findings about specific people. Moreover, practitioners should make every effort to ensure that the data are not used in ways that expose the opinions or actions of individual members. By avoiding the assessment and exposure of individual members, consultants increase trust and cooperation with the diagnosis and enhance their ability to contribute to organizational— as opposed to individual-level—change. Unfortunately, this approach often cannot be applied to heads of units, who are closely identified with their unit's operations and held responsible for its performance by management or outside bodies.

Some practitioners favor a resolution of the politics dilemma that is diametrically opposed to the one just presented. This opposing approach argues that practitioners of diagnosis, like other consultants, owe their loyalties primarily to their clients. This resolution has the advantage of removing consultants from involvement in political processes that are beyond their control. This approach can also simplify the process of defining project goals and priorities. Nonetheless, this resolution may suffer from ethical limitations and may even be unworkable. In practice, it is often very difficult to determine the client to whom the consultant owes loyalty. Is it the person who authorized payment for the study, the individual who first asked for it, those who approved and sponsored it, or those who will receive the feedback and act on it? In many cases, these are different people with divergent needs and interests.

The preceding two resolutions come close to asserting that the solution to the politics dilemma lies in embracing one of the horns of the dilemma: The first approach argues for trying to benefit nearly everyone, whereas the second implies working mainly for the benefit of a specific individual or subgroup. Other partial resolutions seek to chart a middle course between these two poles by coping realistically and directly with the essentially political character of organizations.

One alternative is to seek broad sponsorship and supervision for the diagnosis so that members of the organization assume responsibility for negotiating and resolving many of the power implications of the study. For example, studies of industrial firms can be sponsored and coordinated by committees that include representatives of management and labor (Mirvis & Seashore, 1980). The major drawback of broad sponsorship and supervision of a diagnosis is that it renders the design of the study and data analysis vulnerable to the very political pressures that sponsorship is supposed to overcome.

There is another well-trod path to relieving consultants of the responsibility for solving both the politics and the goals dilemmas (Argyris, 1970; Bowen, 1977). According to this approach, the main obligation of consultants is to provide clients with valid information and allow them the freedom to decide whether and how to act on this information. This approach has the virtue of discouraging consultants from trying to impose their values and recommendations on the client organization and encouraging them to accept the fact that the power and responsibility for acting on diagnostic findings lie with members of the organization and not with the consultant. This approach, however, sometimes leaves unsettled the critical questions of what constitutes valid information and who are the real clients. Therefore, advocates of this view may inadvertently encourage consultants to underestimate the political impact of their work and lead them to blame clients for failure to enact recommendations.

A less elegant but more realistic resolution of the politics dilemma begins with the assumption that consultants are mainly responsible to a limited number of clients, and that these clients need to define a clear set of expectations and priorities for the diagnosis. A first step, therefore, is to require clients, with or without the aid of the consultant, to define study goals and the evaluative criteria to be used, such as the criteria for assessing organizational effectiveness. Next, practitioners can introduce additional criteria that are compatible with client goals and standards. In addition, practitioners may favor problem definitions and solutions that benefit the widest possible range of groups and individuals but fall within the boundaries set by client priorities.

According to this approach, consultants may advocate particular goals and effectiveness criteria and may favor particular solutions to organizational problems. Consultants, however, are restricted to positions compatible with client needs and expectations. Moreover, the final responsibility for interpreting and acting on diagnostic findings lies with the client. A major drawback of this approach is that it can encourage consultants to gear their work too closely to clients' expectations, rather than making a comprehensive and objective assessment of the needs of the client organization. In consequence, practitioners may fail to discover sources of ineffectiveness and routes to organizational improvement besides those their clients have already considered. An additional drawback is that consultants may have to choose among several individuals who assert that they are the "real clients" or among several people who perform part of the role of client.

How, then, should consultants decide who is the appropriate client? One answer is that they should look for a person who has both the authority and the expertise needed to use the diagnosis as a means to organizational improvement. From this standpoint, the ideal client is often the highest executive officer concerned with the operations of the unit under study, usually the CEO or the head of a semiautonomous division. Another possibility is that the ideal client is the head of a functional department, such as human resources, who is assigned responsibility for handling the challenges and problems being examined by the diagnosis.

This way of defining the client helps practitioners decide with whom they should work closely in planning a diagnosis and making recommendations. Practitioners, however, may not know at the outset of a project whether particular functionaries have the power and expertise to interpret diagnostic feedback and implement recommendations successfully. Moreover, this approach requires practitioners to make the strong assumption that their clients can define clear, overriding organizational interests or goals and will act on them. An additional difficulty is that this solution to the politics dilemma effectively excludes subordinate groups, such as labor or community representatives, from participating directly in the definition of project goals or the development of recommendations for action.   ·

In practice, some individuals and groups will usually gain from diagnosis and subsequent changes, whereas others will lose. Hence, consultants and their clients need to confront the politics dilemma to chart a mutually acceptable course of action. If practitioners anticipate the political impact of their work, they may be more able to avoid or cope with opposition to the study or its recommendations.

THE PROFESSIONALISM DILEMMA

This dilemma relates to tensions between strict professional standards and considerations of personal values or self-interest.

Professional Standards Versus Practitioner Interests

One expression of this dilemma is tension between the dictates of professional integrity and practitioners' efforts to market their services, please the client, and maintain professional credibility. In the extreme, this dilemma can boil down to a choice between working to please the client and conducting an honest assessment of the organization. Sometimes consultants discover that clients have asked for a diagnosis to obtain expert approval for steps they have already decided on. These decisions may reflect a pet theory about what is really going on in the organization or the dictates of fashion or expediency. In other instances, clients may simply want to use the diagnosis to ward off critics. In these situations, clients will probably be hostile to negative findings or suggestions that they deviate from their plans or preconceptions.

External consultants can sometimes avoid or terminate projects that involve such threats to honest diagnostic inquiry. But what should internal consultants do if turning down an assignment means risking their jobs? What can internal or external practitioners do if they have committed themselves to conduct a diagnosis before they discover that their client has prejudged the results? In such cases, practitioners can try their best to broaden the approach to the study taken by the client and other members of the organization and strive to promote genuine organizational improvements, rather than serving the client's narrow self-interest.

In other cases, it is even more difficult for practitioners to resolve the tensions between their own interests and their professional obligations and responsibilities. For instance, should practitioners risk using promising but untested models and techniques when these approaches seem appropriate but may not produce the desired results? Should they stick to familiar data-gathering techniques that will produce quick results and make a good impression on clients without contributing much to organizational improvement? Ideally, in such a situation, the practitioner would explain to the clients that the problems cannot effectively be handled with popular, off-the-shelf techniques, and the clients would accept the risks and uncertainties associated with using a newer approach.

A related problem involves practitioners' concerns that they will seem ignorant and lose assignments if they admit that certain consulting assignments lie outside of their areas of specialization. In fact, however, many important organizational issues lie beyond the competencies of consultants trained mainly in general management, social, or behavioral science. Consultants are professionally obligated to disclose these limitations to clients and seek expert help when needed.

Conflict between professional integrity and self-interest may also stem from the tentative and ambiguous status of applied social and behavioral sciences. As researchers, practitioners are aware that using a different measurement technique or a slightly different definition of variables might alter the results of a study. They also realize that diagnostic issues can be framed in a variety of ways, and that there is more than one plausible analysis of the state of an organization and ways to improve it. Similarly, they know that there is limited research evidence in support of many popular interventions and design changes. Can consultants share such imitations and ambiguities with members of the client organization without appearing amateurish and unprofessional?

The answer to this question depends on consultants' relations with clients. If consultants present themselves as science-based experts who possess all the knowledge and tools needed to find a solution to virtually any organizational problem, they will have difficulty admitting such ambiguities. Instead, they can acknowledge that there is only a limited evidence base for many diagnostic explanations and recommendations. Moreover, consulting and management are professions that must cope with high levels of ambiguity and complexity (Weick, 1995). Both managers and consultants can respond to these challenges by continually formulating, checking, and reformulating their analyses and explanations (Schon, 1983). From this vantage point, consultants should encourage clients to confront ambiguities by adopting an experimental attitude based on working hypotheses. A client who adopted such an experimental approach might say something like this: "The diagnosis seems to provide a good understanding of what is causing that problem and some good ideas about what to do about them. Let's try them out to see what happens."

This experimental approach can give rise to systematic tests of the effects of interventions, less rigorous pilot projects, and a more general hypothesis-testing approach to daily affairs. This experimental attitude is illustrated by the manager who decides to test her understanding of the benefits and risks of delegating authority and the conditions necessary for effective delegation. She assigns her subordinates greater responsibility and develops new reporting mechanisms. Then, she examines how delegation is affecting her staff members and her relation to them. In light of this assessment, she adjusts her behavior accordingly.

An additional form of tension between professional obligations and personal interests arises when diagnostic practitioners are tempted to propose more elaborate forms of data gathering and analysis than are strictly needed. They may thereby increase their fees or generate data that can be used in academic research or other consulting projects. In both instances, the same kinds of standards that apply to other consulting professions are appropriate here: Like other professionals, diagnostic practitioners should be encouraged to publish reports of their experiences and findings provided that the consultants do not exploit their clients for this purpose. Likewise, no one would have consultants take vows of poverty before entering the profession. However, they cannot legitimately pursue personal gain in ways that harm their clients or generate unjustified, hidden costs.

Evaluating Diagnostic Projects

A second expression of the professionalism dilemma involves the evaluation of diagnostic projects. Ideally, diagnostic studies, like other forms of organizational interventions, should be subject to evaluation. Otherwise, practitioners cannot legitimately claim that their work is scientific, nor can they systematically improve their work. There are many practical limitations to project evaluation and feedback, however. Sometimes, consultants or clients shy away from project evaluation to escape criticism or avoid drawing attention to disappointing project results. Practitioners often lose contact with their clients after completing a diagnosis. Hence, they cannot obtain meaningful feedback on the project's impact. Even if consultants receive feedback, objective assessment of the results of diagnosis and other forms of consultation is often impossible. Diagnosis forms only one link in a complex chain of actions that must be completed if the client organization is to achieve organizational improvements, which were the ultimate goal of the diagnosis.

The task of evaluating a diagnosis is further complicated by the requirement that consultants not reveal privileged information about clients and their organizations. Evaluation by outside investigators, however, along with criticism and review by peers, is needed for objective evaluation and can greatly contribute to improving diagnostic practice. Practitioners can partially compensate for these weaknesses by conducting their own evaluations. In addition, they may publish accounts of their work in which they disguise the identities of client organizations and deal with the abstract, generic significance of their research and experience (Argyris, 1970).

When it is feasible to evaluate a diagnosis, the evaluative criteria should reflect the goals of the diagnosis and take account of the difficulty of isolating the impact of the diagnosis on the organization. Possible evaluative criteria include the following:

- Perceived usefulness of diagnostic data and information provided to clients and other members

- Extent to which the diagnosis helped clients and members solve specific problems and reduce ineffectiveness

- Contribution of the diagnosis to members' own assessments of their organization's effectiveness

- Perceived usefulness of recommendations

- Degree of use of diagnostic feedback in decision making and action planning

- Degree to which participation in diagnosis and receipt of diagnostic feedback contributes to the clients' capacity for self-assessment, group decision making, and action planning

Preserving Personal Integrity

A third expression of the professional dilemma concerns conflicts between the obligations of practitioners to serve their clients and the practitioners' own personal values and ideals. Diagnostic practitioners, like other professionals, have to develop their own personal standards for deciding whether to accept or decline assignments when conflicts arise between their own values and ethical standards and those embodied in the organization's mission and practices and in its members' behavior. Most consultants would, for example, decline an assignment with a business controlled by an organized crime syndicate. Unfortunately, ethical issues are rarely so clear-cut.

Practitioners should ask themselves, for example, whether from the standpoint of their own values and organizational functioning they want their work to enhance the power of top managers and administrators, who are already powerful and sometimes abuse their power. Some authors (e.g., Alinsky, 1989) have responded to the inequalities of power distribution by advocating use of behavioral science knowledge to assist less powerful groups, such as tenants' unions and block associations in poor neighborhoods. These change agents, however, do not usually gain sufficient access to the organizations they want to influence to be able to conduct diagnostic studies. At the very least, practitioners of diagnosis should be aware of the political implications of their work and their implicit value stances concerning the uses and abuses of power.

The three dilemmas presented here and other ethical difficulties do not lend themselves to optimal, universally applicable solutions. Nonetheless, practitioners can better meet challenges associated with issues such as these by anticipating difficulties before they become intense and highly resistant to resolution. Anticipation of ethical and practice dilemmas also makes it easier for practitioners to align their own expectations and those of influential members of the client organization. These clarifications, which often occur during the entry and contracting stages of diagnosis, reduce subsequent tension over issues such as study objectives; methods of gathering, analyzing, storing, and feeding back sensitive diagnostic data; and the desirability of avoiding attempts to locate and punish problematic employees or groups (Sashkin & Prien, 1996).

CONCLUSION

The success of a diagnosis depends greatly on how practitioners resolve the dilemmas presented here and deal with the analytic, processual, and methodological challenges posed by diagnosis. Practitioners of diagnosis must engage in an elaborate balancing act. They must balance the needs and desires of their clients against those of other stakeholders in the organization and against their own professional understandings of organizational effectiveness. They must also balance the requirements for valid, believable data and analysis against constraints placed on their time and resources and against the need to promote cooperation with the diagnosis and responsiveness to its findings.

To engage in diagnosis is to undertake a difficult but exciting and rewarding task: to help people find out what is going on in their organization and why, while engaged in a complex, changing web of relations; to find a way of serving clients who may be ambivalent about receiving help; to deal with people who may be dead set against the project; to sort among project constraints and a tangle of compelling obligations, values, and professional standards.

NOTES

1. Portions of this chapter draw on Harrison (1990) and are reproduced with permission of *The Journal of Management Consultation*.

2. This discussion expands on Turner's (1982) analysis of consulting goals.

3. The following discussion of the politics and professionalism dilemmas draws in part on Walton and Warwick (1973). For other discussions of professional ethics in consulting, see American Psychological Association (1992); Gellerman, Frankel, and Ladenson (1990); McLean and De Vogel (2002); and Sashkin and Prien (1996).

Appendix A

General Orientation Interview

The orientation interview provides data on important features of a department or unit and major challenges and problems facing it.[1] The numbered sections show the main system features covered and the level of analysis. The questions can be modified so that they better fit specific conditions in the client organization or particular diagnostic issues or apply to divisions or the organization as a whole. An orientation interview can last from 30 minutes to an hour and a half. If time is short or respondents are uncomfortable with sensitive issues, items with asterisks can be left for subsequent interviews or other forms of data gathering.

Before starting, the interviewer explains that the interview is intended to help the consultant learn about what it is like to work in the unit and indicates who is sponsoring the study and will receive feedback. The interviewer explains how the respondent was selected. He or she explains that individual answers are confidential; feedback will refer to responses across interviews, not individual interviews.

GENERAL ORIENTATION INTERVIEW

I. The Person and His or Her Job (Individual Level)

1. Please tell me about your background and your current job (position). (Probe for job title, specialization, previous experience outside and inside the organization, and in the unit in which the person works.)

*2. What is it like to work here? (Probe for feelings about the organization, job, and tasks; e.g., very professional, fun, frustrating, competitive, and worried about reorganization and future employment.)

II. Work Roles, Technology, and Outputs (Group or Higher Level, Depending on Location of Respondent)

1. What are the main outputs of this unit—products, services, and ideas? What units within the organization or outside it receive these outputs?

2. What tasks does your unit (group/department/division/organization) perform? (Probe for task clarity and task problems that are well understood vs. need to develop solutions.) What are the main techniques and technologies used to do these things?

*3. Are there difficulties and barriers to getting work done here or to doing it the way you would like? How can they be overcome?

III. Group Structures and Processes: Controls and Coordinating Mechanisms (Group and Organization Levels)

1. How is work coordinated and controlled within the unit and the organization? (Probe for the kinds of controls used; e.g., budgets, direct supervision, quality control, periodic evaluations, and management by objectives)

*2. Are goals and objectives spelled out for your unit? If so, how? (Probe for the specification of targets vs. general direction and ways in which objectives are specified.)

*3. How do you know when you have done a job well? (Probe for the nature of criteria, type of feedback, and time involved in feedback.)

IV. Environment: Relations to Units Within the Organization (Group and Organization Levels)

*1. What other units do you have to work with to get work done? How are contacts with other units coordinated?

2. What kinds of things does your unit need to get from other units—funds, approval for actions, materials, people, information, etc.? How do you get these things?

3. Are relations to other units pretty smooth and trouble free, or do uncertainties and problems arise? If there are problems, please describe them and explain how they are handled.

V. Environment: External Relations, System Dynamics, and History (Group and Organization Levels)

1. How has the organization (or unit) changed in the past few years?

2. In what markets or fields (areas) does your unit/organization operate (and compete)? What is your organization's position in those markets (or fields)? How is its position changing? (Ask about customers/clients, competitors, revenues, market share, reputation, regulation, funding, and sponsorship.)

*3. What are the main kinds of resources—people, materials, services, funds, and information—that you get from outside organizations and supply to them? On which organizations do you depend the most?

*4. What kinds of things do people in your unit need to know about what is going on outside the organization? How do they find out?

5. Do you run into problems and challenges in obtaining or supplying resources or knowledge? Are there difficulties in dealing with external groups and conditions? If so, please describe them and explain how you handle them.

VI. Structure (Group and Organization Levels)

1. Please describe the formal structure (organization) of your unit and its place in the whole organization. (Probe for job descriptions, unit functions, and reporting relations. If appropriate, ask respondent to draw an organization chart showing the structure of the unit and its relation to the rest of the organization.)

*2. What are the main rules or procedures in your unit that everyone has to follow? How well do they seem to work?

*3 What arrangements exist for taking care of people's health, safety, and retirement needs here?

*4. Are there opportunities for obtaining additional skills or training while working here?

*5. What other (informal) groups and interpersonal ties exist besides the official units? (Probe for work teams, cliques, links between and within departments, groups of employees from similar ethnic backgrounds, etc.)

VII. Processes (Group Level)

1. Who is your supervisor—the person directly responsible for your work? What is it like to work with him or her? *How closely do you work with him or her?

2. How are people rewarded for good work here? (Probe for types of rewards, conditions for receiving them, and feelings about equity.)

*3. How do informal groups and connections affect work in your unit? Do people who belong to different informal groups get along with one another?

*4. How do people find out about what is going on in the unit and the organization as a whole? (Probe for informal and official communication channels and their uses.)

*5. How are decisions made in your unit? What about the organization/division as a whole—how are the decisions made that affect your unit?

*6. How much say do you have in decisions affecting your work? How much does your supervisor consider your opinions or consult you when making decisions that affect you? (Probe for variations by types of decisions.)

*7. Who are the really influential people in your unit? Who really controls what goes on in the organization as a whole?

*8. When people in the unit disagree about things, how are these differences resolved (e.g., boss decides alone, we discuss all the sides of the question until we have the best solution, or we compromise)?

VIII. Culture and Processes (Group and Organization Levels)

1. If you were telling a friend what it was really like to work here, how would you describe the atmosphere? (Probe for staff relations, common practices, norms, beliefs about the nature of the work, how it should be done, and employee's involvement in work.)

2. What do people have to do to get ahead around here? (Probe for kinds of behavior rewarded in the unit and the organization.)

*3. What aspects of work are most emphasized here (e.g., quality, costs, speed, quantity, and innovation)?

*4. Does it pay to take risks or stick your neck out in your unit? (Probe for support for initiative, risk taking, and attitudes toward criticism.)

*5. If you came up with a new idea (e.g., for a service, product, or management improvement), how would your supervisor, your colleagues, and people higher up in the organization react?

6. What is the climate of employee-management relations? Is there a union here? If so, how involved is the union in issues other than salary and benefits? (Probe for union involvement in issues such as changes in job titles and work arrangements.)

IX. Culture and Goals (Group and Organizational Levels)

1. Can you give me an example of one of your unit's major successes or achievements? What about failures? (Probe for criteria for deciding that something succeeded or failed and assumptions about causes.)

*2. What would you say is the overall mission or purpose of your organization? (What does your organization say that it stands for?) How does the organization pursue its mission? (Probe for differences between official and actual purposes.)

*3. Do you feel that your unit and the organization as a whole are operating effectively? What do you mean by effective?

X. Problems and Challenges (Group and Organization Levels)

1. What, in your opinion, are the main strengths of your unit? What are the strengths of the organization as a whole? What are the main weaknesses in the unit? What are the main weaknesses in the organization (or division) as a whole? (Alternative to question about weaknesses: What things seem to be most in need

of change in your unit? What about in the organization as a whole? [Probe for reasons for mentioning these problem areas.])

*2. What do you see as the main challenges facing your unit and organization in the next 2 or 3 years? *Do you have suggestions for how to handle them?

XI. Individual Satisfaction

*1. (If not already evident) In general, how satisfied are you with working here? What things make you feel most satisfied? With what things are you least satisfied?

NOTE

1. This interview draws in part on Burke (1982, pp. 200–202), Levinson (1972, pp. 527–529), and Nadler (1977, pp. 187–191).

Appendix B

Instruments for Diagnosis and Assessment

This appendix lists standardized instruments that have proven useful in diagnostic studies, along with some standardized research instruments that can provide practitioners with useful diagnostic measures and bases for comparisons among organizations. Also described are diagnostic models from which consultants and clients derive instruments that are customized to fit the focal organization. Most of the instruments are self-administered questionnaires. In these instruments, the perceptions, attitudes, and descriptions of respondents are averaged to create group or organizational scores. Consult the sources provided for each instrument for technical information and any user charges or requirements. Permission to use instruments should be obtained from their authors or publishers, and appropriate acknowledgments should be made when using all or part of an existing instrument. Many more scales and instruments are described in academic journals (see Appendix D) or in source books and review articles, such as those by Ashkenasy, Wilderom, and Peterson (2000); Cook, Hepworth, and Wair (1981); Kraut (1996); Lester and Bishop (2001); Price (1997); and Rousseau (1990). Consult subject indices such as ERIC and MEDLINE for instruments tailored to specific types of organizations (e.g., Gershon, Stone, Bakken, & Larson, 2004; Lester & Bishop, 2001; Scott, Mannion, Davies, & Marshall, 2003).

BROAD INSTRUMENTS AND MODELS

The instruments and models discussed in this section cover many areas. Investigators may select among subscales to focus on particular issues or topics.

Organizational Assessment Inventory (OAI)

The Organizational Assessment Inventory (OAI; Van de Ven & Ferry, 1980) is a family of questionnaires that provide sophisticated, sometimes complex, data at the individual, unit, divisional, and organizational levels (see Chapter 3). The instrument has been used in many basic and applied research investigations.

Substantial evidence has accumulated for the reliability, construct validity, and predictive validity of scales constructed from OAI items (Gresov, 1989; Van de Ven & Chu, 1989; Van de Ven & Walker, 1984). For additional information and a list of studies that have used the OAI, contact Andrew Van de Ven, 3M Professor of Human Systems Management, Carlson School of Management, University of Minnesota, Minneapolis, MN 55455; e-mail: avandeven@csom.umn.edu.

Michigan Organizational Assessment Questionnaire

The Michigan Organizational Assessment Questionnaire (MOAQ; Cammann, Fichman, Jenkins, & Kelsh, 1983) covers a wide range of individual-, group-, and organization-level variables (see Chapter 3) and has provided a basis for the development of many subsequent organizational surveys. See Seashore, Lawler, Mirvis, and Cammann (1983) for information on other instruments in the Michigan Quality of Work Life Program.

Organizational Assessment Survey

This instrument was developed by the U.S. Office of Personnel Management to provide government agencies with a standardized tool for assessing organizational strengths and weaknesses, planning training and change programs, and making comparisons across time and among agencies (benchmarking). The survey has been used by many federal agencies and some states. It covers employee perceptions in 17 areas of organizational climate, including rewards, training, innovation, consumer orientation, teamwork, communication, performance, supervision, and diversity. It can be administered over the Internet or in a paper-and-pencil version. See Muldrow, Schay, and Buckley (2002); go to http://www.opm.gov/employ/html/org_asse.asp; or contact Brigette Schay, director of assessment services, Division for HR Products and Services, U.S. Office of Personnel Management (e-mail: bwschay@opm.gov).

Organizational Fitness Profiling

Organizational Fitness Profiling (OFP) is a process that helps a top management team align its organization (internal system) with its strategy. OFP has been used to identify barriers to implementing business strategy and plan organizational redesign to enhance strategy implementation (Beer & Eisenstat, 1996; Beer, Eisenstat, & Biggadike, 1996). OFP links organizational goals (objectives and business strategy) with organizational capabilities (coordination, competence, commitment, communication, conflict management, creativity, and capacity management). These in turn are linked to organizational levers (leadership team, work system, management processes, human resource system, principles and culture, and corporate context). OFP data are collected through open interviews conducted by members of a task force within the focal organization. See www.orgfitness.com for details and applications.

Burke-Litwin Model and Survey

This popular systems model (Burke & Litwin, 1992) specifies 11 areas that shape organizational performance, as reported by participants. These are grouped into transformational (i.e., macro) factors (environment, mission and strategy, leadership, and culture) and transactional factors (structure, management practices, policies and procedures, work unit climate, task requirements, motivation, and individual needs and values). The survey derived from the model (Burke, Coruzzi, & Church, 1996) contains standard questions and items tailored to the client organization and the diagnostic problems.

FOCUSED INSTRUMENTS AND MODELS

The instruments and models discussed in this section focus on one or more system elements or features.

Human Resources Scorecard

This research-based model (Becker, Huselid, & Ulrich, 2001) provides a guide to assessing alignment between a firm's human resource function and its strategy implementation system. The model identifies human resource activities that drive or enable performance and thereby contribute to strategy implementation. The scorecard data are typically extracted from existing records about human resource management (e.g., the proportion of merit pay that is determined by performance and training hours for new employees). See Walker and Randall (2001) for an application of the scorecard instrument. Human resources consulting firms offer proprietary consulting and data management services based on this popular assessment model.

National Organizations Survey

This research-oriented survey (Kalleberg, Spaeth, Marsden, & Knoke, 1996) was designed to provide data on human resource practices in 1,002 work establishments in the United States. The instrument concentrates on staffing, training, use of contingent contracts, high-performance work organization, incentives, and benefits. There is also coverage of formal structure, employee background characteristics, environment, productivity, and performance. For the database, see Kalleberg, Marsden, and Knoke (2001) and http://www. icpsr .umich.edu:8080/ICPSR-STUDY/03190.xml.

Culture Audits

The Kilmann-Saxton Culture Gap Survey (Kilmann & Saxton, 1983) examines actual and desired work group norms about task support, task innovation, social relationships, and personal freedom. Closing gaps is expected to improve performance (Kilmann, 1985). Harrison and Stokes (1992) provide sets of statements for characterizing 15 facets of culture. Other culture audits have been developed to assess compatibility of firms planning mergers (e.g., http:// www.lsolowassociates.com/MainPages/Strategy/CultureAudit.html).

Team Diagnostic Survey

Team Diagnostic Survey is a questionnaire in which members of a work team report on how the team is structured, supported, and led. The instrument measures concepts contained in Hackman's Action Model for Group Task Performance (see Chapter 4) and subsequently developed in Hackman (2002). It also provides an assessment of how well members work together and measures of their motivation and satisfaction. Details are provided at http://www .wjh.harvard.edu/~tds/.

Instruments for Organization Development and Team Building

See the annual publications of the Pfeiffer group (e.g., Biech, 2004) for short questionnaires for use in these activities. Most of these questionnaires have not been validated for research purposes.

Multifactor Leadership Questionnaire

This widely used and well-developed instrument (http://www.mindgarden .com/Assessments/mlq.htm; Avolio, Bass, & Jung, 1999) provides measures of the degree to which both top-level and midlevel managers use transactional leadership (i.e., results-oriented management) and transformational leadership (i.e., using power to empower others to realize the leader's organizational vision). Applicable to both public- and private-sector organizations, measures of leadership have been shown to be correlated with a range of measures of organizational effectiveness (Yukl, 2001).

Appendix C

A Guide to Diagnosing Behavior During Meetings

This guide rests on the premise that many factors affect group performance and effectiveness, and there is no universal set of processes that is best for all types of tasks and all combinations of group composition, technology, and organizational context (see Chapter 3). Hence, the questions that follow direct attention to important group processes while allowing practitioners to draw their own conclusions about the importance and impact of each factor. Because the questions are merely guides to observations, they do not provide instructions about what particular behaviors to note or how to make inferences from them. To answer each of these diagnostic questions, observers must consult their notes on behavior observed during the meeting (e.g., shouting), decide what generalizations they can make about these observations (e.g., members often shout at one another), and make appropriate inferences from the observations (e.g., shouting shows that members take differences of opinion personally rather than focusing mainly on the task at hand). Users can select questions, modify them, and apply them to fit the particular features of the observed group and relevant effectiveness criteria. In addition to guiding observations, these questions can provide a framework for feedback. The guide can also be used by groups wishing to engage in self-diagnosis.

QUESTIONS ABOUT GROUP MEETINGS

1. Goals, Targets, and Procedures

Are the goals of the meeting or the problems to be dealt with stated in advance? Are clear guidelines given for the time and resources to be devoted toward reaching these ends? Do participants understand and accept the goals and purposes of the meeting and the group, or do they seem to have different, hidden agendas for the meeting?

2. Participation

Do participants other than the leader share in developing goals and guidelines for the meeting? Do most people participate, or do a few talk most of the time?

How much airing of divergent views occurs? Do participants have the time and ability to examine the information they are given? Are they prepared for the discussion?

3. Flow of Information and Ideas

Are there opportunities for clarification and development of the ideas and proposals presented? Are ideas and proposals adequately summarized so that participants can keep track of their progress? How much does the chair guide and control the discussion? Does discussion shift easily from one topic to another, or must these shifts be forced by the leader or a few participants?

4. Problem Solving

Do participants define clearly the problems facing them and search for alternative solutions before making decisions? Do they weigh alternatives and take dissenting opinions seriously, or do they slip into groupthink, in which everyone backs one solution without seriously discussing others? Do they consider long-term consequences of actions in addition to short-term ones? Do participants draw on and learn from past experiences? Do they consider new ideas and solutions to problems as well as familiar, time-tested ones?

5. Decision Making

What kinds of procedures do participants use to decide on proposals: ignoring them, acceptance or rejection by top managers, decision by a minority of powerful participants, voting, or consensus? Do participants seem to accept these methods? Do these methods seem to produce the best decisions? Do important issues go undecided?

6. Conflict

What important conflicts arise during the meeting? Do conflicts stimulate thinking and problem solving or disrupt the meeting? How are conflicts handled—by someone forcing a solution, one party backing down, bargaining, or collaborating on a mutually satisfying solution? What are the effects of relying on these methods (e.g., do members seem anxious to work together or passive and alienated)?

7. Interpersonal Relations and Feelings

How cohesive is the group? Are there opportunities for enhancing group solidarity? How do participants react to differences in other people's social and personal backgrounds, work experience, and areas of expertise? Do they respect or even value such differences, or do some forms of diversity make it more difficult for participants to work together? Do they discuss differences of opinion in terms of common standards and values, or do they treat differences as personal conflicts? Do members seem to trust one another? Do they listen to one another or interrupt and ignore others?

8. Outcomes

Do participants find the meetings satisfying or frustrating? What are the major outcomes of the meeting: solutions, decisions, proposals, ideas, and so on? Are implications for action spelled out clearly, including responsibilities for executing them, time, staff, and resources allotted for doing so, and forms of follow-up and evaluation? How satisfied are participants, leaders, and outside stakeholders with these outcomes? How well do the outcomes fit other relevant effectiveness criteria (e.g., innovativeness and adaptiveness)?

To decide how important each of the listed items is to group functioning and whether a particular feature, such as participation in decision making, impacts group effectiveness, practitioners will have to trace the feature's impact on specific indicators of effectiveness. Consider the question of whether participants share in developing goals and guidelines for action. If consultants define the satisfactions and feelings of group members as important indicators of effectiveness, participation in goal setting may indeed facilitate effectiveness. If speed of decision making is the evaluative criterion, then participation in goal setting may reduce effectiveness. The context in which the group operates is also important. Consider cross-functional teams: A team within a private firm that is supposed to develop a new service line may accept that management sets broad goals and milestones for them; team members will probably expect to develop their own operational objectives and procedures. In contrast, participants in a similar team in a more authoritarian context, such as the military, may more readily accept having most of their operational objectives and procedures set from above.

Appendix D

Resources for Developing Expertise in Diagnosis

ACADEMIC TRAINING

Social and behavioral science departments of universities and professional schools offer courses on organizations and organizational behavior that can equip students with useful methods and conceptual frames. Some programs also provide a few courses on applied research, organization development, change management, and consulting. Many schools of management offer concentrations in organizational behavior and human resource management. Courses in statistics and quantitative research techniques are widely offered. An increasing number of professional schools also offer some training in qualitative research techniques, such as unstructured observation and open interviewing. These methods, however, are more often taught in departments of anthropology, sociology, and psychology.

WORKSHOPS AND CONFERENCES

Many universities offer evening courses that are more oriented toward practice than are courses for credit. Workshops, seminars, conferences, and publications on a wide range of relevant topics are also sponsored by professional and academic organizations, including the following:[1]

- Academy of Management (http://www.aomonline.org) (The Organizational Change and Development Division and the Management Consulting Division are of particular interest.)
- American Management Association (http://www.amanet.org)
- American Society for Training and Development (http://www.astd.org)
- American Sociological Association, Section on Organizations, Occupations, and Work (http://www.asanet.org/sections/oow.html)
- European Association of Work and Organizational Psychology (http://www.tuta.hut.fi/eawop)
- International Association of Applied Psychology, Division of Work and Organizational Psychology (http://www.iaapsy.org)

- International Association of Human Resource Information Management (http://www.ihrim.org)
- National Training Laboratories for Applied Behavioral Sciences (http://www.ntl.org)
- Organization Development Institute (http://www.odinstitute.org)
- Organization Development Network (http://www.odnetwork.org)
- Society for Human Resource Management (http://www.shrm.org)
- Society for Industrial and Organizational Psychology, Division 14 of the American Psychological Association (http://siop.org)

The Web sites of these organizations contain links to publications and other useful sites. Readers outside the United States should also consult the Web sites of academic, applied research, and consulting associations and firms in their home countries and in specific industries or fields. Readers may also wish to inquire about workshops and training programs offered by local consulting firms specializing in applied behavioral science and change management. Names of local firms may be obtained from university professors who specialize in organizational research, listings under management consultants in the Yellow Pages, and listings such as Gale Research Group (2004) and the registries of the Organization Development Network and the Organization Development Institute.

FURTHER READING

Those who want to read further about fields such as organizational behavior, human resource management, diagnosis, and organization development can begin with basic texts (Bolman & Deal, 2003; Cummings & Worley, 2001; Daft, 2004; Gordon, 2002; Harrison & Shirom, 1999; Morgan, 1996) and handbooks (Anderson, Ones, Sinangil, & Viswesvaran, 2001; Baum, 2002; Rogelberg, Church, Waclawskii, & Stanton, 2002) and consult the references in these books. The Web sites of several commercial publishers, including Addison-Wesley, Elsevier, Jossey-Bass, and Sage Publications, list many monographs and collections in areas such as applied research, organizational change, consultation, and organization development.

The following periodicals and annuals include material that may be of use to practitioners:

Academic Journals

Academy of Management Journal

Academy of Management Review

Administrative Science Quarterly
Human Resource Management
Journal of Applied Behavioral Science
Journal of Applied Psychology
Personnel Psychology

Research Annuals

Annual Review of Psychology
Annual Review of Sociology
Research in Organizational Behavior
Research in Organizational Change and Development
Research in Sociology of Organizations

Management and Practice-Oriented Periodicals

Academy of Management Executive
Annual: Developing Human Resources
Business Week
Fortune
Harvard Business Review
Organizational Dynamics
Sloan Management Review

NOTE

1. This listing and those that follow are not intended to apply approval of any specific course, publication, or program. See Waclawski and Church (2002) for more information on some of the groups listed here.

References

Abrahamson, E. (1996). Management fashion. *Academy of Management Review, 21,* 254–285.

Abrahamson, E., & Fairchild, G. (1999). Management fashion: Lifecycles, triggers, and collective learning processes. *Administrative Science Quarterly, 44*(4), 653–863.

Adler, N., & Bartholomew, S. (1992). Managing globally competent people. *Academy of Management Executive, 6*(3), 52–65.

Ajzen, I. (2001). Nature and operation of attitudes. *Annual Review of Psychology, 52,* 27–58.

Alinsky, S. (1989). *Rules for radicals: A pragmatic primer for realistic radicals* (Rev. ed.). New York: Vintage.

American Psychological Association. (1992). Ethical principles of psychologists and code of conduct. *American Psychologist, 47,* 1597–1611.

Anderson, N., Ones, D., Sinangil, H., & Viswesvaran, C. E. (Eds.). (2001). *Handbook of industrial, work, & organizational psychology* (Vol. 2). Thousand Oaks, CA: Sage.

Andrews, K. (1980). *The concept of corporate strategy* (Rev. ed.). Homewood, IL: Dow-Jones/Irwin.

Argyris, C. (1970). *Intervention theory and method.* Reading, MA: Addison-Wesley.

Argyris, C., & Schon, D. (1995). *Organizational learning II: Theory, method, and practice* (2nd ed.). Reading, MA: Addison-Wesley.

Ashkenasy, N., Wilderom, C., & Peterson, M. (Eds.). (2000). *Handbook of organizational culture and climate.* Thousand Oaks, CA: Sage.

Austin, M. (1982). *Evaluating your agency's programs.* Beverly Hills, CA: Sage.

Avolio, B. J., Bass, B., & Jung, D. (1999). Reexamining the components of transformational and transactional leadership using the multifactor leadership questionnaire. *Journal of Occupational and Organizational Psychology, 72,* 441–462.

Bartlett, C., & Ghoshal, S. (1990). Matrix management: Not a structure, a frame of mind. *Harvard Business Review, 68*(4), 138–145.

Bartunek, J., & Louis, M. R. (1988). The interplay of organization development and transformation. *Research in Organizational Change and Development, 2,* 97–134.

Baum, J. (Ed.). (2002). *Blackwell companion to organizations.* Oxford, UK: Blackwell.

Becker, B., Huselid, M., & Ulrich, D. (2001). *The HR scorecard: Linking people, strategy, and performance.* Boston: Harvard Business School Press.

Beckhard, R. (1969). *Organization development: Strategies and models.* Reading, MA: Addison-Wesley.

Beckhard, R., & Harris, R. (1975). Strategies for large system change. *Sloan Management Review, 16,* 43–55.

Beckhard, R., & Harris, R. (1977). *Organizational transitions: Managing complex change.* Reading, MA: Addison-Wesley.

Beer, M. (1980). *Organizational change and development—A systems view.* Santa Monica, CA: Goodyear.

Beer, M., & Eisenstat, R. (1996). Developing an organization capable of implementing strategy and learning. *Human Relations, 49*(5), 597–619.

Beer, M., Eisenstat, R., & Biggadike, E. R. (1996). Developing an organization capable of strategy implementation and reformulation. In B. Moingen & A. Edmonson (Eds.), *Organizational learning and competitive advantage* (pp. 16–184). Thousand Oaks, CA: Sage.

Beer, M., Eisenstat, R., & Spector, B. (1990). *The critical path to corporate renewal.* Boston: Harvard Business School Press.

Beer, M., & Nobria, N. (2000). Resolving the tension between theories E and O of change. In M. Beer & N. Nobria (Eds.), *Breaking the code of change* (pp. 1–34). Boston: Harvard Business School Press.

Berenson, A. (2004, February 7). Survey finds profit pressure is leading to poor decisions. *New York Times,* p. B3.

Biech, A. (2004). *The 2004 Pfeiffer annual: Consulting.* San Francisco: Jossey-Bass.

Block, P. (1981). *Flawless consulting.* San Diego, CA: University Associates.

Block, P. (2000). *Flawless consulting: A guide to getting your expertise used* (2nd ed.). San Francisco: Jossey-Bass/Pfeiffer.

Bluedorn, A., & Lundgren, E. (1993). A culture-match perspective for strategic change. *Research in Organizational Change and Development, 7,* 137–179.

Bolman, L., & Deal, T. (2003). *Reframing organizations: Artistry, choice, and leadership* (3rd ed.). New York: Wiley.

Bowditch, J., & Buono, A. (1989). *Quality of work life assessment* (2nd ed.). Boston: Auburn.

Bowen, D. (1977). Value dilemmas in organization development. *Journal of Applied Behavioral Science, 13,* 543–556.

Bowen, D., & Lawler, E. (1992). The empowerment of service workers: What, why, how, and when. *Sloan Management Review, 33*(3), 31–39.

Brass, D., & Burkhardt, M. (1993). Potential power and power use: An investigation of structure and behavior. *Academy of Management Journal, 36,* 441–470.

Bridges, W. (1991). *Managing transitions: Making the most of change* (2nd ed.). Cambridge, MA: Perseus.

Brown, S., & Eisenhardt, K. (1997). The art of continuous change: Linking complexity theory and time-paced evolution in relentlessly shifting organizations. *Administrative Science Quarterly, 42,* 1–34.

Bunker, B. B., & Alban, B. (2002). Understanding and using large system interventions. In J. Waclawski & A. Church (Eds.), *Organization development: A data-driven approach to organizational change* (pp. 222–241). San Francisco: Jossey-Bass.

Buono, T., & Bowditch, J. (1989). *The human side of mergers and acquisitions: Managing collisions between people, cultures, and organizations.* San Francisco: Jossey-Bass.

Burke, W. (1982). *Organization development.* Boston: Little, Brown.

Burke, W. (1993). *Organizational development: A process of learning and changing* (2nd ed.). Reading, MA: Addison-Wesley.

Burke, W., Coruzzi, C., & Church, A. (1996). The organizational survey as an intervention for change. In A. Kraut (Ed.), *Organizational surveys: Tools for assessment and change* (pp. 41–66). San Francisco: Jossey-Bass.

Burke, W. W., & Litwin, G. H. (1992). A causal model of organizational performance and change. *Journal of Management, 18*(3), 523–545.

Cameron, K. (1980). Critical questions in assessing organizational effectiveness. *Organizational Dynamics, 9,* 66–80.

Cameron, K. (1984). The effectiveness of ineffectiveness. *Research in Organizational Behavior, 6,* 235–285.

Cameron, K. (1994). Strategies for successful organizational downsizing. *Human Resource Management, 33,* 189–211.

Cameron, K., Freeman, H., & Mishra, A. (1991, August). Best practices in white-collar downsizing: Managing contradictions. *Academy of Management Executive, 5,* 57–73.

Cameron, K., & Quinn, R. E. (1988). Organizational paradox and transformation. In K. Cameron & R. E. Quinn (Eds.), *Paradox and transformation: Toward a theory of change in organization and management* (pp. 1–18). Cambridge, MA: Ballinger.

Cameron, K., Sutton, R., & Whetten, D. (1988). Issues in organizational decline. In K. Cameron, R. Sutton, & D. Whetten (Eds.), *Readings in organizational decline: Frameworks, research, and prescriptions* (pp. 3–19). Cambridge, MA: Ballinger.

Cammann, C., Fichman, M., Jenkins, G., & Kelsh, J. (1983). Assessing the attitudes and perceptions of members. In S. Seashore et al. (Eds.), *Assessing organizational change* (pp. 71–138). New York: Wiley.

Campbell, D. (1977). On the nature of organizational effectiveness. In J. Pennings (Ed.), *New perspectives on organizational effectiveness* (pp. 13–55). San Francisco: Jossey-Bass.

Cartwright, S., & Cooper, C. (1993). The role of cultural compatibility in successful organizational marriage. *Academy of Management Executive, 7*(2), 57–70.

Champy, J. (1995). *Reengineering management: The mandate for new leadership.* New York: Harper.

Chin, R., & Benne, K. (1985). General strategies for effecting changes in human systems. In W. Bennis, K. Benne, & R. Chin (Eds.), *The planning of change* (4th ed., pp. 22–45). New York: Holt, Rinehart and Winston.

Church, A. H., & Waclawski, J. (1998). *Designing and using organizational surveys.* Aldershot, UK: Gower.

Clemons, E., Thatcher, M., & Row, M. (1995). Identifying sources of reengineering failures: A study of behavioral factors contributing to reengineering risk. *Journal of Management Information Systems, 12,* 9–26.

Connolly, T., Conlon, E., & Deutsch, S. (1980). Organizational effectiveness: A multi-constituency approach. *Academy of Management Review, 5,* 211–217.

Cook, J., Hepworth, S. T., & Wair, P. (1981). *Experience of work: A compendium and review of 249 measures and their use.* New York: Academic Press.

Cook, T., Campbell, D., & Peracchio, L. (1991). Quasi-experimentation. In M. Dunnette & L. Hough (Eds.), *Handbook of industrial and organizational psychology* (2nd ed., pp. 491–576). Palo Alto, CA: Consulting Psychologists Press.

Cooper, C. L. (1998). *Theories of organizational stress.* New York: Oxford University Press.

Cummings, T., & Worley, C. (2001). *Organization development and change* (7th ed.). Cincinnati, OH: South-Western.

Daft, R. (2004). *Organization theory and design* (8th ed.). Mason, OH: Thomson/ South-Western.

Danna, K., & Griffin, R. W. (1999). Health and well-being in the workplace: A review and synthesis of the literature. *Journal of Management, 25,* 357–384.

Davenport, T. (1993). *Process innovation: Reengineering work through information technology.* Boston: Harvard Business School Press.

Davis, S., Lawrence, P., Kolodny, H., & Beer, M. (1977). *Matrix.* Reading, MA: Addison-Wesley.

Denison, D. (1996). What is the difference between organizational culture and organizational climate? A native's point of view on a decade of paradigm wars. *Academy of Management Review, 21,* 619–654.

Denison, D., Hart, S., & Kahn, J. (1996). From chimneys to cross-functional teams: Developing and validating a diagnostic model. *Academy of Management Journal, 39,* 1005–1023.

Denison, D., & Mishara, A. (1995). Toward a theory of organizational culture and effectiveness. *Organization Science, 6,* 204–223.

Denison, D., & Spreitzer, G. (1991). Organization culture and organizational development: A competing values approach. *Research in Organizational Change and Development, 5,* 1–21.

Denzin, N., & Lincoln, Y. (Eds.). (2000). *Handbook of qualitative research* (2nd ed.). Thousand Oaks, CA: Sage.

Donaldson, T., & Preston, L. (1995). The stakeholder theory of the corporation: Concepts, evidence, and implications. *Academy of Management Review, 20,* 85–92.

Dougherty, D. (2002). Grounded theory research methods. In J. Baum (Ed.), *Blackwell companion to organizations* (pp. 849–866). Oxford, UK: Blackwell.

Duncan, J., Ginter, P., & Swayne, L. (1998, August 3). Competitive advantage and international organizational assessment. *Academy of Management Executive, 12,* 6–16.

Dunphy, D., & Stace, D. (1988). Transformational and coercive strategies for planned organizational change: Beyond the OD model. *Organization Studies, 9,* 317–334.

Enz, C. (1989). The measurement of perceived intraorganizational power: A multi-respondent perspective. *Organization Studies, 10,* 241–251.

Faletta, S., & Combs, W. (2002). Surveys as a tool for organization development. In J. Waclawski & A. Church (Eds.), *Organization development: A data-driven approach to organizational change* (pp. 78–102). San Francisco: Jossey-Bass.

Ferlie, E., & Shortell, S. (2001). Improving the quality of health care in the United Kingdom and the United States: A framework for change. *Milbank Quarterly, 79,* 281–315.

Finkelstein, S. (1992). Power in top management teams: Dimensions, measurement and validation. *Academy of Management Journal, 35,* 505–538.

Fisher, C., & Locke, E. (1992). The new look in job-satisfaction research and theory. In C. Cranny, P. Smith, & E. Stone (Eds.), *Job satisfaction: How people feel about their jobs and how it affects their performance* (pp. 165–194). New York: Lexington Books.

Ford, J., & Baucus, D. (1987). Organizational adaptation to performance downturns: An interpretation-based perspective. *Academy of Management Review, 12,* 366–380.

Freeman, H., Dynes, R., Rossi, P., & Whyte, W. (Eds.). (1983). *Applied sociology*. San Francisco: Jossey-Bass.

Frost, P., & Egri, C. (1991). The political process of innovation. *Research in Organizational Behavior, 13,* 229–295.

Fry, R. (1982). Improving trustee, administrator, and physician collaboration through open systems planning. In M. Plovnick et al. (Eds.), *Organization development: Exercises, cases and readings* (pp. 282–292). Boston: Little, Brown.

Galbraith, J. (1977). *Organization design*. Reading, MA: Addison-Wesley.

Galbraith, J., Lawler, E., & Associates. (1993). *Organizing for the future: The new logic for managing complex system*. San Francisco: Jossey-Bass.

Galbraith, J. R. (2002). *Designing organizations: An executive guide to strategy, structure, and process*. San Francisco: Jossey-Bass.

Gale Research Group. (2004). *Consultants and consulting organizations directory* (27th ed.). Detroit, MI: Author.

Gellerman, W., Frankel, M., & Ladenson, R. (1990). *Values and ethics in organization and human systems development*. San Francisco: Jossey-Bass.

Gershon, R., Stone, P., Bakken, S., & Larson, E. (2004). Measurement of organizational culture and climate. *Journal of Nursing Administration, 34,* 33–40.

Ghoshal, S., & Bartlett, C. (1990). The multinational corporation as in interorganizational network. *Academy of Management Review, 15,* 603–625.

Goodman, P., & Pennings, J. (1980). Critical issues in assessing organizational effectiveness. In E. Lawler et al. (Eds.), *Organizational assessment* (pp. 185–215). New York: Wiley.

Gordon, J. (2002). *Organizational behavior: A diagnostic approach* (7th ed.). Upper Saddle River, NJ: Prentice Hall.

Gormley, W., & Weimer, D. (1999). *Organizational report cards*. Cambridge, MA: Harvard University Press.

Greenbaum, T. (1998). *The handbook for focus group research* (2nd ed.). Thousand Oaks, CA: Sage.

Greiner, L., & Schein, V. (1988). *Power and organization development: Mobilizing power to implement change*. Reading, MA: Addison-Wesley.

Gresov, C. (1989). Exploring fit and misfit with multiple contingencies. *Administrative Science Quarterly, 34,* 431–453.

Grey, C., & Mitev, N. (1995). Re-engineering organizations: A critical appraisal. *Personnel Review, 24,* 6–18.

Guzzo, R., & Dickson, M. (1996). Teams in organizations: Recent research on performance and effectiveness. *Annual Review of Psychology, 46,* 307–338.

Hackman, J., & Wageman, R. (1995). Total quality management: Empirical, conceptual and practical issues. *Administrative Science Quarterly, 40,* 309–342.

Hackman, J. R. (1987). The design of work teams. In J. Lorsch (Ed.), *Handbook of organizational behavior*. Englewood Cliffs, NJ: Prentice Hall.

Hackman, J. R. (Ed.). (1991). *Groups that work (and those that don't)*. San Francisco: Jossey-Bass.

Hackman, J. R. (2002). *Leading teams: Setting the stage for great performances*. Boston: Harvard Business School Press.

Hamel, G., & Prahalad, C. (1994). *Competing for the future.* Boston: Harvard Business School Press.

Hammer, M., & Champy, J. (1993). *Reengineering the corporation: A manifesto for business revolution.* New York: Harper.

Harrison, M. (1990). Hard choices in diagnosing organizations. *Journal of Management Consulting, 6*(1), 13–21.

Harrison, M. (1991). The politics of consulting for organizational change. *Knowledge and Policy, 4,* 92–107.

Harrison, M. (2004). *Implementing change in health systems: Market reforms in the United Kingdom, Sweden, and The Netherlands.* London: Sage.

Harrison, M., & Shirom, A. (1999). *Organizational diagnosis and assessment: Bridging theory and practice.* Thousand Oaks, CA: Sage.

Harrison, R., & Stokes, H. (1992). *Diagnosing organizational culture.* San Francisco: Pfeiffer.

Hausser, C., Pecorella, P., & Wissler, A. (1975). *Survey guided development: A manual for consultants.* Ann Arbor: University of Michigan, Institute for Social Research.

Hayes, R., & Abernathy, W. (1980). Managing our way to economic decline. *Harvard Business Review, 58,* 67–77.

Heijltjes, M. G. (2000). Advanced manufacturing technologies and HRM policies: Findings from chemical and food and drink companies in The Netherlands and Great Britain. *Organization Studies, 21,* 775–805.

Heijltjes, M. G., & van Witteloostuijn, A. (1996). *Configurations of market environments, competitive strategies, manufacturing technologies, and human resource policies: A two-industry and two-country analysis of fit* (Report No. NIBOR/RM/96/07). University of Maastricht, Maastricht, The Netherlands. Retrieved from http://www-edocs.unimaas.nl/files/nib96007.pdf

Hennestad, B. (1988). Inculture: The organizational culture of INC. In S. Tyson, K. F. Ackermann, M. Domsch, & P. Joynt (Eds.), *Appraising and exploring organisations.* London: Croom Helm.

Higgs, A., & Ashworth, S. (1996). Organizational surveys: Tools for assessment and research. In A. Kraut (Ed.), *Organizational surveys: Tools for assessment and change* (pp. 19–40). San Francisco: Jossey-Bass.

Howard, A., & Associates. (Eds.). (1994). *Diagnosing for organizational change: Methods and models.* New York: Guilford.

Hoyle, R., Harris, M., & Judd, C. (2001). *Research methods in social relations* (7th ed.). Belmont, CA: Wadsworth.

Huber, G., & Glick, W. (1993). What was learned about organization change and redesign. In G. Huber & W. Glick (Eds.), *Organizational change and redesign: Ideas and insights for improving performance* (pp. 383–392). New York: Oxford University Press.

Ibarra, H. (1993). Network centrality, power, and innovation involvement: Determinants of technical and administrative roles. *Academy of Management Journal, 136,* 471–501.

Institute of Medicine. (2001). *Crossing the quality chasm: A new health system for the 21st century.* Washington, DC: National Academy Press.

Jackson, S. E., & Schuler, R. (1995). Understanding human resource management in the context of organizations and their environments. *Annual Review of Psychology, 46,* 237–264.

Jayaram, G. (1976). Open systems planning. In W. Bennis et al. (Eds.), *The planning of change* (3rd. ed., pp. 275–283). New York: Holt, Rinehart and Winston.

Jick, T. (1979). Mixing qualitative and quantitative methods: Triangulation in action. *Administrative Science Quarterly, 24,* 602–611.

Jimenez, J., Escalante, J., & Aguirre-Vazquez, J. (1997). Application of the search conference methodology to planning in higher education. *System Practices, 10,* 255–271.

Kalleberg, A., Marsden, P., & Knoke, D. (2001). *National Organizations Survey (NOS), 1996–1997* (Computer file, ICPSR version, Minneapolis: University of Minnesota Center for Survey Research [producer], 1997). Inter-University Consortium for Political and Social Research [distributor].

Kalleberg, A., Marsden, P., Spaeth, J., & Knoke, D. (1996). *Organizations in America: Analyzing their structure and human resource practices.* Thousand Oaks, CA: Sage.

Kanter, R. (1979). Power failure in management circuits. *Harvard Business Review, 57,* 65–75.

Kanter, R., & Brinkerhoff, D. (1981). Organizational performance. *Annual Review of Sociology, 7,* 321–349.

Kanter, R., Stein, B., & Jick, T. (1992). *The challenge of organizational change: How companies experience it and leaders guide it.* New York: Macmillan.

Kaplan, R. S., & Norton, D. P. (1996). *The balanced scorecard: Translating strategy into action.* Boston: Harvard Business School Press.

Katz, D., & Kahn, R. (1978). *The social psychology of organizations* (2nd ed.). New York: Wiley.

Katz, H. C., Kochan, T., & Weber, M. (1985). Assessing the effects of industrial relations systems and efforts to improve the quality of working life on organizational effectiveness. *Academy of Management Journal, 28,* 509–526.

Keen, P. (1990). Telecommunications and organizational choice. In J. Fulk & C. Steinfeld (Eds.), *Organizations and communication technology* (pp. 295–312). Newbury Park, CA: Sage.

Kerr, S. (1995). On the folly of rewarding A, while hoping for B. *Academy of Management Executive, 9,* 7–14.

Kilmann, R. (1985). Five steps for closing culture gaps. In R. Kilmann, M. Saxton, R. Serpa, & Associates (Eds.), *Gaining control of the corporate culture* (pp. 351–369). San Francisco: Jossey-Bass.

Kilmann, R., Covin, T., & Associates (Eds.). (1988). *Corporate transformations: Revitalizing organizations for a competitive world.* San Francisco: Jossey-Bass.

Kilmann, R., & Saxton, M. (1983). *Kilmann-Saxton Culture-Gap Survey (A).* Pittsburgh, PA: Organizational Design Consultants.

King, G., Keohane, R., & Verba, S. (1994). *Designing social inquiry: Scientific inquiry in qualitative research.* Princeton, NJ: Princeton University Press.

Kinnear, T., & Taylor, J. (1995). *Marketing research: An applied approach* (5th ed.). New York: McGraw-Hill/Irwin.

Kizer, K. (1999, January/February). The "new VA": A national laboratory for health care quality management. *American Journal of Medical Quality, 14,* 13–20.

Kolb, D., & Frohman, A. (1970). An organization development approach to consulting. *Sloan Management Review, 12,* 51–65.

Kotter, J., & Schlesinger, L. (1979). Choosing strategies for change. *Harvard Business Review, 57,* 106–114.

Kraut, A. (1996). *Organizational surveys: Tools for assessment and change.* San Francisco: Jossey-Bass.

Lawler, E., & Drexler, J. (1980). Participative research: The subject as co-researcher. In E. Lawler et al. (Eds.), *Organizational assessment* (pp. 535–547). New York: Wiley.

Lawler, E., Nadler, D., & Mirvis, P. (1983). Organizational change and the conduct of organizational research. In S. Seashore, E. Lawler, P. Mirvis, & C. Cammann (Eds.), *Assessing organizational change* (pp. 19–48). New York: Wiley.

Leach, J. (1979). The organizational history: A consulting analysis and intervention tool. In G. Gore & R. Wright (Eds.), *The academic consultant connection* (pp. 62–69). Dubuque, IA: Kendall/Hunt.

Lee, R., & Fielding, N. (1998). *Computer analysis and qualitative research.* Thousand Oaks, CA: Sage.

Lester, P., & Bishop, K. (2001). *Handbook of tests and measurement in education and the social sciences* (2nd ed.). Lancaster, PA: Technomic.

Levinson, H. (1972). *Organizational diagnosis.* Cambridge, MA: Harvard University Press.

Levinson, H. (1994). The practitioner as a diagnostic instrument. In A. Howard & Associates (Eds.), *Diagnosis for organizational change: Methods and models* (pp. 27–52). New York: Guilford.

Levinson, H. (2002). *Organizational assessment: A step-by-step guide to effective consulting.* Washington, DC: American Psychological Association.

Lewin, A., & Minton, J. W. (1986). Determining organizational effectiveness: Another look and an agenda for research. *Management Science, 32*(5), 514–538.

Lofland, J., & Lofland, L. (1995). *Analyzing social settings: A guide to qualitative observation and analysis* (3rd ed.). Belmont, CA: Wadsworth.

Lusthaus, C., Adrien, M. H., Anderson, G., Carden, F., & Montvalvan, G. (2002). *Organizational assessment: A framework for improving performance.* Washington, DC: Inter-American Development Bank.

Lynam, P., Smith, T., & Dwyer, J. (1994, June). Client flow analysis: A practical management technique for outpatient settings. *International Journal for Quality in Health Care, 6*(2), 179–186.

Macy, B., & Izumi, H. (1993). Organizational change, design, and work innovations: A meta-analysis of 131 North American field studies, 1961–1991. *Research in Organizational Change and Development, 7,* 235–313.

Mainero, L. (1986). Coping with powerlessness: The relationship of gender and job dependency to empowerment-strategy usage. *Administrative Science Quarterly, 31,* 633–653.

Majchrzak, A. (1984). *Methods for policy research.* Beverly Hills, CA: Sage.

Maslach, C., Schaufeli, W., & Leiter, M. (2001). Job burnout. *Annual Review of Psychology, 52,* 397–422.

McCracken, G. (1988). *The long interview.* Newbury Park, CA: Sage.

McKinley, W. (1993). Organizational decline and adaptation: Theoretical controversies. *Organization Science, 4,* 1–19.

McLean, G., & De Vogel, S. (2002). Organization development ethics: Reconciling tensions in OD values. In J. Waclawski & A. Church (Eds.), *Organization development: A data-driven approach to organizational change* (pp. 302–320). San Francisco: Jossey-Bass.

McMahan, G. C., & Woodman, R. W. (1992). The current practice of organization development within the firm: A survey of large industrial corporations. *Group and Organization Management, 117,* 117–134.

Meyer, A., Tsui, A., & Hinnings, C. (1993). Configurational approaches to organizational analysis. *Academy of Management Journal, 36,* 1175–1195.

Miles, M., & Huberman, A. (1994). *Qualitative data analysis: An expanded sourcebook of new methods* (2nd ed.). Thousand Oaks, CA: Sage.

Miller, D., & Salkind, N. (Eds.). (2002). *Handbook of research design and social measurement.* Thousand Oaks, CA: Sage.

Milliken, F., & Martins, L. (1996). Searching for common threads: Understanding the multiple effects of diversity in organizational groups. *Academy of Management Review, 21,* 402–433.

Mintzberg, H. (1979). *The structuring of organizations.* Englewood Cliffs, NJ: Prentice Hall.

Mintzberg, H. (1983). *Power in and around organizations.* Englewood Cliffs, NJ: Prentice Hall.

Mintzberg, H. (1994). *The rise and fall of strategic planning.* New York: Free Press.

Mintzberg, H., Lampel, J., Quinn, J. B., & Ghoshal, S. (2003). *The strategy process* (4th ed.). Englewood Cliffs, NJ: Prentice Hall.

Mirvis, P., & Seashore, S. (1980). Being ethical in organizational research. In E. Lawler et al. (Eds.), *Organizational assessment* (pp. 583–612). New York: Wiley.

Moch, M., Cammann, C., & Cooke, R. (1983). Organizational structure: Measuring the degree of influence. In S. Seashore, E. Lawler, P. Mirvis, & C. Cammann (Eds.), *Assessing organizational change* (pp. 177–202). New York: Wiley.

Morgan, G. (1988). *Riding the waves of change: Developing managerial competencies for a turbulent world.* San Francisco: Jossey-Bass.

Morgan, G. (1996). *Images of organization* (2nd ed.). Thousand Oaks, CA: Sage.

Muldrow, T., Schay, B., & Buckley, T. (2002). Creating high-performing organizations in the public sector. *Human Resource Management, 41*(3), 341–354.

Nadler, D. (1977). *Feedback and organization development: Using data-based methods.* Reading, MA: Addison-Wesley.

Nadler, D., & Lawler, E. (1983). Quality of work life: Perspectives and directions. *Organizational Dynamics, 11*(3), 20–30.

Nadler, D., & Shaw, R. (1995). Change leadership: Core competency for the twenty-first century. In D. Nadler, R. Shaw, A. Walton, & Associates (Eds.), *Discontinuous change: Leading organizational transformation* (pp. 3–13). San Francisco: Jossey-Bass.

Nadler, D., Shaw, R., Walton, A., & Associates. (1995). *Discontinuous change: Leading organizational transformation.* San Francisco: Jossey-Bass.

Nadler, D., & Tushman, M. (1980). A congruence model for diagnosing organizational behavior. In E. Lawler et al. (Eds.), *Organizational assessment* (pp. 261–278). New York: Wiley.

Nadler, D., & Tushman, M. (1989). Leadership for organizational change. In A. Mohrman, S. Mohrman, G. Ledford, T. Cummings, & E. Lawler (Eds.), *Large scale organizational change* (pp. 110–119). San Francisco: Jossey-Bass.

Neill, T., & Mindrum, C. (2000). Human performance that increases business performance: The growth of change management and its role in creating new forms of business value. In M. Beer & N. Nohria (Eds.), *Breaking the code of change* (pp. 339–360). Boston: Harvard Business School Press.

Nelson, R., & Mathews, K. M. (1991). Cause maps and social network analysis in organizational diagnosis. *Journal of Applied Behavioral Science, 27,* 379–397.

Nelson, R. E. (1988). Social network analysis as an intervention tool. *Group and Organization Studies, 13,* 39–58.

Neuendorf, K. (2002). *The content analysis guidebook.* Thousand Oaks, CA: Sage.

Nutt, P. (2001). De-development as a way to change contemporary organizations. *Research in Organizational Change and Development, 13,* 81–115.

O'Mahoney, S., & Barley, S. (1999). Do digital telecommunications affect work and organization? The state of our knowledge. *Research in Organizational Behavior, 21,* 125–161.

Orton, J., & Weick, K. (1990). Loosely coupled systems: A reconceptualization. *Academy of Management Review, 15,* 203–223.

Osborn, R., & Baughn, C. (1993). Societal considerations in the global technological development of economic institutions: The role of strategic alliances. *Research in the Sociology of Organizations, 11,* 113–150.

Pascale, T. (1984, Spring). Perspectives on strategy: The real story behind Honda's success. *California Management Review,* 47–72.

Patton, M. (1999). *User-focused evaluation* (3rd ed.). Thousand Oaks, CA: Sage.

Perkins, D., Nadler, D., & Hanlon, M. (1981). A method for structured naturalistic observation of organizational behavior. In J. Pfeiffer & J. Jones (Eds.), *The 1981 annual handbook for group facilitators* (pp. 222–244). San Diego, CA: University Associates.

Peters, T., & Waterman, R. (1982). *In pursuit of excellence.* New York: Harper & Row.

Pfeffer, J. (1981). *Power in organizations.* Marshfield, MA: Pitman.

Pfeffer, J. (1992). *Managing with power: Politics and influence in organizations.* Boston: Harvard Business School Press.

Pfeffer, J., & Salancik, G. (2003). *The external control of organizations.* Palo Alto, CA: Stanford University Press.

Plovnick, M., Fry, R., & Burke, W. (1982). *Organization development: Exercises, cases, and readings.* Boston: Little, Brown.

Porras, J., & Robertson, P. (1987). Organization development theory: A typology and evaluation. *Research in Organizational Change and Development, 1,* 1–57.

Porras, J., & Robertson, P. (1992). Organization development: Theory, research, and practice. In M. Dunnette & L. Hough (Eds.), *Handbook of organizational and industrial psychology* (2nd ed., Vol. 3, pp. 719–822). Palo Alto, CA: Consulting Psychologists Press.

Porras, J., & Silver, R. (1991). Organization development and transformation. *Annual Review of Psychology, 42,* 51–78.

Porter, L., Allen, R., &. Angle, H. (1981). The politics of upward influence in organizations. *Research in Organizational Behavior, 3,* 109–150.

Porter, M. (1996, November/December). What is strategy. *Harvard Business Review, 74,* 61–78.

Porter, M. (1998a). *Competitive advantage: Creating and sustaining superior performance.* New York: Free Press.

Porter, M. (1998b). *Competitive strategy: Techniques for analyzing industries and competitors.* New York: Free Press.

President and Fellows of Harvard College. (1980). *Action planning and implementation: A manager's checklist.* Boston: HBS Case Service.

Price, J. (1997). Handbook of organizational measurement. *International Journal of Manpower, 18*(4–6), 305–558.

Quinn, J. B. (1980). *Strategies for change: Logical incrementalism.* Homewood, IL: Irwin.

Quinn, R. E., & Cameron, K. (1983). Organizational life cycles and shifting criteria of effectiveness: Some preliminary evidence. *Management Science, 3,* 33–51.

Quinn, R. E., & Rohrbaugh, J. (1983). A spatial model of effectiveness criteria: Toward a competing values approach to organizational analysis. *Management Science, 29,* 363–377.

Ramanujam, R. (2003). Effects of discontinuous change on latent errors in organizations: The moderating role of risk. *Academy of Management Journal, 46*(5), 608–617.

Ramirez, I. L., & Bartunek, J. (1989). The multiple realities and experiences of organization development consultation in health care. *Journal of Organizational Change Management, 2*(1), 40–57.

Rashford, N., & Coghlan, D. (1994). *The dynamics of organizational levels: A change framework for managers and consultants.* Reading, MA: Addison-Wesley.

Reason, J. (1997). *Managing the risks of organizational accidents.* Aldershot, UK: Ashgate.

Reason, P. (1984). Is organization development possible in power cultures? In A. Kakabadse & C. Parker (Eds.), *Power politics and organizations: A behavioral science view* (pp. 185–202). Chichester, UK: Wiley.

Robbins, S. P. (1978). Conflict management and conflict resolution are not synonymous terms. *California Management Review, 21,* 67–75.

Rogelberg, S., Church, A., Waclawski, J., & Stanton, J. (2002). Organizational survey research. In S. G. Rogelberg (Ed.), *Handbook of research methods in industrial and organizational psychology* (pp. 141–160). Maiden, MA: Blackwell.

Romanelli, E., & Tushman, M. (1994). Organizational transformation as punctuated equilibrium: An empirical test. *Academy of Management Journal, 37,* 1141–1166.

Rossi, P., Freeman, H., & Lipsey, M. (1999). *Evaluation: A systematic approach* (6th ed.). Thousand Oaks, CA: Sage.

Rossi, P., & Whyte, W. F. (1983). The applied side of sociology. In H. Freeman, R. Dynes, P. Rossi, & W. F. Whyte (Eds.), *Applied sociology* (pp. 5–31). San Francisco: Jossey-Bass.

Rousseau, D. (1985). Issues of level in organizational research: Multi-level and cross-level perspectives. *Research in Organizational Behavior, 7,* 1–37.

Rousseau, D. (1990). Assessing organizational culture: The case for multiple methods. In B. Schneider (Ed.), *Climate and culture* (pp. 153–192). San Francisco: Jossey-Bass.

Rousseau, D. (1997). Organizational behavior in the new organizational era. *Annual Review of Psychology, 48,* 515–546.

Rubenstein, D., & Woodman, R. (1984). Spiderman and the Burma Raiders: Collateral organization theory in action. *Journal of Applied Behavioral Science, 20,* 1–21.

Salancik, G., & Pfeffer, J. (1977). An examination of need satisfaction models of job attitudes. *Administrative Science Quarterly, 22,* 427–456.

Sashkin, M., & Prien, E. (1996). Ethical concerns and organizational surveys. In A. Kraut (Ed.), *Organizational surveys: Tools for assessment and change* (pp. 381–403). San Francisco: Jossey-Bass.

Savage, G., Nix, T., Whitehead, C., & Blair, J. (1991). Strategies for assessing and managing organizational stakeholders. *Academy of Management Executive, 5,* 61–75.

Schaffer, R. (1988). *The breakthrough strategy.* New York: Harper.

Schein, E. (1997). *Organizational culture and leadership* (2nd ed.). San Francisco: Jossey-Bass.

Schein, E. (1998). *Process consultation revisited: Building the helping relationship.* Englewood Cliffs, NJ: Prentice Hall.

Schilit, W., & Locke, E. (1982). A study of upward influence in organizations. *Administrative Science Quarterly, 27,* 304–316.

Schon, D. (1983). *The reflective practitioner: How professionals think in action.* New York: Basic Books.

Schon, D., & Rein, M. (1994). *Frame reflection: Toward the resolution of intractable controversies.* New York: Basic Books.

Scott, J. (2000). *Social network analysis: A handbook* (2nd ed.). Thousand Oaks, CA: Sage.

Scott, T., Mannion, R., Davies, H., & Marshall, M. (2003). The quantitative measurement of organizational culture in health care: A review of the available instruments. *Health Services Research, 38*(3), 923–945.

Seashore, S., Lawler, E., Mirvis, P., & Cammann, C. (Eds.). (1983). *Assessing organizational change.* New York: Wiley.

Selingo, J. (2003, November 6). Footing the bill for computer lab. *New York Times,* p. E1.

Senge, O. (1994). *The fifth discipline: The art and practice of the learning organization.* New York: Doubleday.

Sherman, S. (1995, December 11). Wanted: Company change agents. *Fortune, 132*(12), 197–198.

Shirom, A. (1983). Toward a theory of organizational development interventions in unionized work settings. *Human Relations, 36,* 743–764.

Shirom, A. I. (2003). The effects of work-related stress on health. In M. Schabracq, J. Winnbust, & C. Cooper (Eds.), *Handbook of work and health psychology* (2nd ed., pp. 63–83). New York: Wiley.

Spreitzer, G. (1996). Social structural characteristics of psychological empowerment. *Academy of Management Journal, 39,* 483–504.

Stanton, J., & Rogelberg, S. (2001, July). Using internet/intranet web pages to collect organizational research data. *Organizational Research Methods, 4,* 200–217.

Starbuck, W. (1992). Learning by knowledge-intensive firms. *Journal of Management Studies, 29*(6), 713–740.

Steele, F. (1973). *Physical settings and organization development.* Reading, MA: Addison-Wesley.

Stewart, D. (1992). *Secondary research: Information sources.* Newbury Park, CA: Sage.

Stone, E. (1992). A critical analysis of social information processing models of job perceptions and job attitudes. In C. J. Cranny, P. Smith, & E. Stone (Eds.), *Job satisfaction: How people feel about their jobs and how it affects their performance* (pp. 21–44). New York: Lexington Books.

Strauss, G. (1976). Organization development. In R. Dubin (Ed.), *Handbook of work, organization, and society* (pp. 617–685). Chicago: Rand McNally.

Sussman, G. (1990). Work groups: Autonomy, technology, and choice. In P. Goodman, L. A. Sproull, & Associates (Eds.) *Technology and organizations* (pp. 87–108). San Francisco: Jossey-Bass.

Sutherland, J. (Ed.). (1978). *Management handbook for public administrators.* New York: Van Nostrand.

Sutton, S. (1998). Predicting and explaining intentions and behavior: How well are we doing. *Journal of Applied Social Psychology, 28*(15), 1317–1338.

Taylor, S. E. (1991). Asymmetrical effects of positive and negative events: The mobilization-minimization hypothesis. *Psychological Bulletin, 110,* 67–85.

Thomas, K., & Velthouse, B. (1990). Cognitive elements of empowerment: An "interpretive" model of intrinsic task motivation. *Academy of Management Review, 15,* 666–681.

Thompson, J. D. (1967). *Organizations in action.* New York: McGraw-Hill.

Tichy, N. (1983). *Managing strategic change: Technical, political, and cultural dynamics.* New York: Wiley.

Tichy, N., & DeVanna, M. (1997). *The transformational leader: The key to global competitiveness* (2nd ed.). New York: Wiley.

Trice, H., & Beyer, J. (1993). *The cultures of work organizations.* Englewood Cliffs, NJ: Prentice Hall.

Trochim, W. (2001). *The research methods knowledge base* (2nd ed.). Cincinnati, OH: Atomic Dog.

Tsui, A. (1990). A multiple-constituency model of effectiveness: An empirical examination at the human resource subunit level. *Administrative Science Quarterly, 35,* 458–484.

Tsui, A. (1994). Reputational effectiveness: Toward mutual responsiveness framework. *Research in Organizational Behavior, 16,* 257–307.

Turner, A. (1982). Consulting is more than giving advice. *Harvard Business Review, 60,* 120–129.

Tushman, M., & Nadler, D. (1978). Information processing as an integrative concept in organizational design. *Academy of Management Review, 3,* 613–624.

Vaill, P. (1989). *Managing as a performing art: New ideas for a world of chaotic change.* San Francisco: Jossey-Bass.

Van de Ven, A., & Chu, Y. (1989). A psychometric assessment of the Minnesota Innovation Survey. In A. Van de Ven, H. L. Angle, & M. S. Poole (Eds.), *Research on the management of innovation* (pp. 55–103). New York: Harper & Row.

Van de Ven, A., & Drazin, R. (1985). The concept of fit in contingency theory. *Research in Organizational Behavior, 7,* 333–365.

Van de Ven, A., & Ferry, D. (1980). *Measuring and assessing organizations.* New York: Wiley.

Van de Ven, A., & Poole, M. S. (2002). Field research methods. In J. Baum (Ed.), *Blackwell companion to organizations* (pp. 867–888). Oxford, UK: Blackwell.

Van de Ven, A., & Walker, G. (1984). The dynamics of inter-organizational coordination. *Administrative Science Quarterly, 29*(4), 598–621.

Waclawski, J., & Church, A. (2002). Introduction and overview of organizational development as a data-driven approach for organizational change. In *Organization development: A data-driven approach to organizational change* (pp. 3–26). San Francisco: Jossey-Bass.

Waclawski, J., & Rogelberg, S. (2002). Interviews and focus groups: Quintessential organization development techniques. In J. Waclawski & A. Church (Eds.), *Organization development: A data-driven approach to organizational change* (pp. 103–126). San Francisco: Jossey-Bass.

Walker, G., & Randall, J. (2001, Winter). Designing and implementing an HR scorecard. *Human Resource Management, 40*(4), 365–377.

Walton, R. (1975). Quality of working life: What is it? *Sloan Management Review, 15,* 11–21.

Walton, R., & Warwick, D. (1973). The ethics of organization development. *Journal of Applied Behavioral Science, 9,* 681–698.

Webb, E., Campbell, D., Schwartz, R., & Seechrest, L. (1966). *Unobtrusive measures: Non-reactive research in the social sciences.* Chicago: Rand McNally.

Weber, R. P. (1990). *Basic content analysis* (2nd ed.). Newbury Park, CA: Sage.

Weick, K. (1985). Systematic observational methods. In G. Lindzey & A. Aronson (Eds.), *Handbook of social psychology* (3rd ed., Vol. 2, pp. 567–634). Reading, MA: Addison-Wesley.

Weick, K. (1995). *Sensemaking in organizations.* Thousand Oaks, CA: Sage.

Weick, K., & Quinn, R. (1999). Organizational change and development. *Annual Review of Psychology, 50,* 361–386.

Weick, K., & Sutcliffe, K. M. (2001). *Managing the unexpected: Assuring high performance in an age of complexity.* San Francisco: Jossey-Bass.

Weisbord, M. (1978). *Organizational diagnosis: A workbook of theory and practice.* Reading, MA: Addison-Wesley.

Weisbord, M. (1988). Toward a new practice theory of OD: Notes on snapshooting and moviemaking. *Research in Organization Change and Development, 2,* 59–96.

Weitzel, W., & Jonsson, E. (1989). Decline in organizations: A literature integration and extension. *Administrative Science Quarterly, 34,* 91–109.

Weitzel, W., & Jonsson, E. (1991). Reversing the downward spiral: Lessons from W. T. Grant and Sears Roebuck. *Academy of Management Executive, 5*(3), 7–22.

Worren, N., Ruddle, K., & Moore, K. (1999). From organizational development to change management: The emergence of a new profession. *Journal of Applied Behavioral Science, 35*(3), 273–286.

Yin, R. (2002). *Case study research: Design and methods* (3rd ed.). Thousand Oaks, CA: Sage.

Yukl, G. (2001). *Leadership in organizations* (5th ed.). Upper Saddle River, NJ: Prentice Hall.

Zammuto, R. (1984). A comparison of multiple constituency models of organizational effectiveness. *Academy of Management Review, 9,* 606–616.

Index